From Glory into Glory

From Called to Sent Series, Book 6

From Glory into Glory

Elizabeth Moreau

From Called to Sent Series, Book 6

The From Called to Sent Series
Adult Discipling Curriculum

Book 1   *I'm Saved, So What?*
Book 2   *I Believe... Something!*
Book 3   *Pray Then in This Way*
Book 4   *The Will of The Father*
Book 5   *Sufficient Grace*
Book 6   *From Glory into Glory*

With all my love…

in honor of

Mom & Dad

*with deep gratitude for the privilege
of watching you strive daily
to live like Christ.*

Copyright © Elizabeth Moreau 2020

All rights reserved. No part of this book may be reproduced or transmitted in any form or by any means, electronic or mechanical, including photocopying, recording, or by any information storage or retrieval system, without the permission in writing from the publisher. For information, contact Servants' Feast Press.

Second edition.

Scripture taken from the HOLY BIBLE, NEW INTERNATION VERSION. Copyright 1973, 1978, 1984 International Bible Society. Used by permission of Zondervan Bible Publishers.

Published by Servants' Feast Press
Kingwood, Texas, USA

ISBN: 978-1-7334141-1-1

www.servantsfeast.org

Contents

	Introduction	xi
I.	The Last Prayer before Death	1
II.	Growing Up in Salvation	25
III.	Entering the Promised Land	51
IV.	The Eight Vices: Physical	77
V.	The Eight Vices: Spiritual	99
VI.	The Darkness before Dawn	131
VII.	From Glory into Glory	150

Introduction

After a long and intense struggle with faithfulness and discipleship, the question was posed to me, "Why did you not tell me it would be so hard? Why has no one ever told me how hard it is to be a fully committed disciple?" Interesting question. I am not too sure there is an easy answer, although my first inclination is to be flippant, something to the effect of, *"No one ever mentions it because it so rarely happens with any intentionality."* In other words, while some people truly grow in depth of faith and willing obedience, sadly, the majority of us stagnate, moving from one church project to the next and taking one Bible study after another. What is it exactly that grows a mature Christian?

In the case above, a great deal of waiting and insecurity bordering on terror preceded abiding peace with Jesus Christ and the clear pathway forward in Christ. Dying to self and trusting in God sound so much simpler on paper. The reality turns out to be far harder. When Jesus first called His disciples, He did not mention the difficulties that lay ahead either for Him or, eventually, for them. He invited them to, "Come and see."[1] That is much the same invitation we all receive. Come and see. The reasonable explanation for Jesus' failure to explain the potential consequences was because the outcome was dependent upon the interest in and obedience of each disciple. If one quit along the way, he would never know nor understand the fullness of the life to which he was called, nor would he have cause to wonder about the personal cost of following Jesus Christ.

What I hope for readers to gain through this book is some insight into those things – those actions, attitudes, values, events, and circumstances – that provide fertile ground for growth in Christian life and faith. I know of no systematic pathway to mature discipleship, no "follow these steps and you will be a spiritual powerhouse" sort of manual. Rather, maturation as a Christian occurs in much the same manner as does emotional or intellectual maturation, one day at a time in and through the people, places, and proceedings of daily life. God works in our lives through the people He places there, or allows to

---

[1] cf. John 1:39.

be there, the ever-changing circumstances in which we are situated, and the experiences to which He leads us, as well as those that are thrown at us from the world in which we live. The primary factor in growing as a Christian has more to do with determination to be a faithful child of our Father than it does with some sort of plan of growth. God works in mysterious ways, and certainly, His ways are higher than our ways, as His thoughts are higher than our thoughts.[2] We are wise to let Him grow us as He sees fit in His wisdom and lead us with His patience and love rather than overeagerly try to mature ourselves.

The following chapters do not attempt to provide a map to follow for being a good Christian. Rather, they are intended to give us a glimpse into the struggles, promises, and challenges of faithfulness at a profound depth. We have much to face, much to experience. Just as Jesus' disciples had no idea what lay ahead of them, neither do we know what direction our life will take in the days, months, and years ahead. The thing about it is, the disciples would never have seen so many astonishing and awe-inspiring events if they had not followed Jesus Christ when He called. Moreover, they never would have reached the astounding accomplishments of life as an apostle had they worried about possible difficulties as His follower. They became men who no doubt surprised themselves. From mere fishermen to evangelists traveling thousands of miles around the ancient world, eleven of the twelve men Jesus invited to "Come and see" did exactly that. They came and saw God heal the sick, make the blind to see, the lame to walk, and the dead to rise. Jesus did not tell them they would see those things either. He simply said, "Come and see."

Beyond what they saw, what the disciples themselves eventually *did* was certainly more than they ever imagined. Born with the expectation of dying where they lived, these men became vessels of the Holy Spirit, doing what Jesus did – preaching and teaching, healing, casting out demons, bringing the dead to life, and more – as they took the Gospel of Jesus Christ to the ends of the known world. These men, who had no plan for their lives beyond fishing and the like in the tiny area into which they were born, were used mightily by their Father in ways beyond any feasible expectation they might have had when Jesus said, "Come and see." By following Him, they became themselves. They

---

[2] cf. Isaiah 55:9.

became more alive, more filled with purpose, stronger, braver, and more courageous than they had imagined possible before they were filled with the Holy Spirit. That is what it means to become ourselves – for all that prevents us from being really and truly alive to be defeated, so that we might be unleashed in glorious freedom to accomplish great things for our Father and His Kingdom and to be the catalyst and agent of changed lives. As were the ordinary disciples, *we* will be astounded at whom we become and what we do.

The richest of lives is purchased at a high cost. I hope to help you, the reader, be aware of what is required to become a fully alive Christian, a little christ in the world, as well as how that might come to you or what might be asked of you. The book is hardly exhaustive. Who can count all the ways God works with each of us individually, much less define them? But having an idea of what is expected and ways to strive to move God as He leads us to Himself hopefully will ease the shock that comes when we are intentional about growing up in our salvation. Growing and maturing in Jesus Christ is hard, but the reward is worth it not only in the next life, but also in this life here and now. To live without fear, to love with abandon, to give without first counting is an unrestrained life full of possibility for good and filled with the purposes of the Kingdom. One never lacks a reason to get out of bed in the morning because every day holds the promise and the reality of life well lived, an adventure in the making leading to the eternal adventure that is the Kingdom of the Father and the Son and the Holy Spirit.

As you read and study, I pray your heart will hunger for Christ and your soul will thirst for the life that He alone offers. As you pursue faithfulness, may all the Spirit gives come to you in abundance beyond measure.

EM

May 2020

I
The Last Prayer before Death

Some Things We Ought to Know

Transformation and growth in discipleship are hard. I am not sure we are honest about that, or, perhaps, we have forgotten just how much change will occur if we follow Jesus Christ. When we decide to be a disciple – not a believer, but a disciple – we are separating ourselves from the values, priorities, and standards of the world and are moving into a new life drawn from Christ's Kingdom's values, priorities, and standards. Everything we are and everything we know must be adjusted to this new life; we must be changed from the old person into the new person, and sometimes, that is not only unpleasant but painful. One thing we need to realize is that this transformation is often scary. Anyone who has ever moved to a new location knows the unrest that comes with starting a new life elsewhere. Who will be our friends? Where will we buy groceries? What physician will we find? Who will cut our hair? Many of our worries seem trivial, but when the whole of life is changing, the cumulative effect of the unknown generates a measure of fear, no matter how excited we are about the move.

This fear is intensified when our movement is spiritual, intellectual, and psychological. When we are taking risks by learning new ways of being and living, when we begin making different choices based on what we believe we are being asked to do, and our hope and trust is in an invisible God, inevitably, we run up against a wall of fear. What if all that I confess I believe is not *completely* true? What if God really will not come to my rescue? What happens if I take this leap of faith with my whole life and discover that God is not actually there to catch me? We can know in our minds that our thoughts are not accurate, but when the moment comes and we step out on faith, the uncertainty and the waiting can be terrifying. *Is God paying attention?*

The purpose of this book is to help Christians understand some of the contours of growth and movement in the life of a disciple. Moving "from called to sent" requires a great deal of faith and change, all of which is for our blessing ultimately but seldom feels like a blessing in the moment. Being able to recognize the work of the Spirit when it is occurring is reassuring and comforting. Knowing that some of these times through which all disciples pass are normal and are a movement toward life and joy is helpful. Everyone takes his own journey in growth and transformation. No one journey is exactly like another. However, many of the steps we will take individually have been taken by every disciple who has gone before us. No one bounces happily into the Kingdom of God without the pain and death of leaving the world behind, and realizing that you are not the first to be afraid or to doubt is important for sustaining you when you reach crossroads and must choose between journeying in the world and journeying with Christ. Know this as well: you will not be the last either.

Everyone must move from a starting place toward a new destination without a clear pathway between the two. This journey is predicated upon the leading and guidance of the Holy Spirit Who is notoriously hard to pin down. As Jesus Himself pointed out, "The wind blows wherever it pleases. You hear its sound, but you cannot tell where it comes from or where it is going. So it is with everyone born of the Spirit."[3] This is the unknown to which I am referring. We are not geared toward such uncertainty, but as we come to know, truly know deep within our bones, that God is trustworthy and will not fail us, our uncertainty gives way to radical freedom. While our next step may be uncertain, God is absolutely certain, and we are secure in and safe with Him. This is the adventure in abundant joy, blessing, meaning, and purpose for which we were created.

In the illustration above about moving, the ever-present uncertainty of the Hebrews wandering in the desert after the Exodus out of Egypt speaks to us. Worry, fear, and doubt abound throughout the story. Sin and failure are evident repeatedly. But we must remember: the One Who proves Himself in the desert is not the Hebrews, it is God. He has to show Himself to be trustworthy and able to provide and protect. Sure, the Hebrews complained and whined and frequently wanted to turn tail and run back to Egypt, but they did not know God. They worshipped Him and maintained their identity as Hebrews in Egypt – maybe because they were slaves by birth – but they did not know Him well enough to trust Him. So it is with us as well. We believe and desire the greater

---

[3] John 3:8.

things of God, but learning to trust Him is just as complicated for us as it was for the Hebrews. Discipleship is a relationship that grows, and every relationship deepens with trust. The only way for us to come to trust God personally is for Him to meet us individually in our own personal desert and prove to us that He is trustworthy. The hard part for us is simply being in the desert and waiting. As He did with Jesus, the Spirit will lead us there, and the desert is finally a place of great blessing in spite of how miserable it might feel at the time. The desert is the place where God reveals His great love for each of us individually and proves that He is trustworthy and will not fail us.

This time of relational development between the Triune God and each of us will occur in the life of every disciple. The only way in which we will know that God is trustworthy is for us to go through a time in the desert where God either comes to our rescue or He does not. We do not have to be afraid of the desert, but neither do we have to enjoy it. One day, each of us will look back on our time of wandering in the wilderness and be grateful. That will be the time and place when our relationship with Jesus Christ began to transition from a superficial belief and simplistic trust to a deep and abiding fellowship with Him through His Spirit. During this period of time and in whatever circumstances that define our wilderness experience, the things in which we have always trusted will call us back to slavery in Egypt. Each of us will have to decide whether we want to move toward the Promised Land or return to Egypt. Recognizing the desert for what it is enables us to see God's hand in the situation and gives us the opportunity to choose to trust Him and let Him provide.

Daily Reflection and Meditation

Some Things We Ought to Know

Can you think of a time in your life when you felt lost and were not sure God was hearing your prayers? What did you do, and what was the outcome?

_____
_____
_____
_____
_____

Looking back on your life, do you think there were times you were in the desert being asked to move and to trust God, but did not recognize it at the time? Ask the Holy Spirit to remind you of such occasions if you cannot think of one. What happened at that time?

_____
_____
_____
_____
_____

Think of other occasions and events in your life when you saw the providence and guidance of God only in retrospect. How did the realization of His presence and work in your life even when you did not know it affect your relationship with Him?

_____
_____

The Last Prayer before Death

The Seed Experience

The Apostle John recorded Jesus saying, "I tell you the truth, unless a kernel of wheat falls to the ground and dies, it remains only a single seed. But if it dies, it produces many seeds."[4] Jesus was speaking of His pending Crucifixion - that He must die to give life to the rest of us. Christ Jesus died for the life of the whole world. Yet, what He says about Himself applies to us in our own lives as well. We, too, must die if we are to rise to new life in Christ and produce fruit for the Kingdom. This emphasis on death throughout the Gospel, first Christ's death then our own, is hard to accept and difficult to understand. Why is death such an issue in Christian life and faith?

The world in which we live is ruled by death. Everyone dies. Likewise, each human being is infected with the death of God's original intentions for the human creature through the sinful nature that destroys our true humanity. The death to which the Gospel calls us is the death of death. We must die to this world of death, to our sinful nature, and rise to eternal life in the midst of, and in spite of, the death into which we were born. This is the whole point of Christianity: the dying to this world and rising to eternal life in Jesus Christ by the power of the Holy Spirit. We are led to death in order to live, truly and fully live. The death we die is to what is false and inhuman. We die to what is wrong, to sin and evil. We die to all that harms us and is destructive of our humanity. Because life and death are opposed to each other, we cannot embrace both at the same time. Yet, because this world and this life are what we know, we do not want to let them go. Indeed, this life is of paramount importance to us precisely because it is all we know. But this life and this world lead to death. The life that Christ is offering is eternal and flows from His Kingdom of life and light. What we know and cling to are a shadow of all that God wants to give us. As Paul wrote, "No eye has seen, no ear has heard, no mind has conceived what God has prepared for those who love Him…"[5] Still, to trade what we know for the promise of something unseen – however wonderful that promise is – is nearly impossible to do. For this reason, we are led to death by the Holy Spirit, to spiritual, intellectual, and psychological

---

[4] John 12:24.
[5] 1 Corinthians 2:9.

death. We are, like the seed, buried in the dark where the old is destroyed and the new is born.

Within every seed is an embryo, and it lies dormant until the seed is buried. Seeds are planted below the surface into the darkness of the earth. For the seed to morph into a plant, it requires both warmth and water appropriate to the thing that it is to become. Water causes the seed and casing to burst, thus, destroying the seed, but germination begins. Sufficient nutrients already exist within the embryo, dormant until the seed breaks open and receives water. At that time a tiny plant begins to spring forth from the germinated embryo. The plant is usually bent as if growing downward even as it pushes toward the light and warmth above the ground. In this state the plant breaks through the crust of the earth and starts to straighten, stretching toward the warmth of the sun. Eventually, the plant's stem will produce tiny branches, then buds, and finally, blossoms, which produce more seeds – be they grains of wheat, apples, or flowers. The single seed that was buried was long destroyed, but its destruction led to the production of many more.

Our death is not unlike the process through which an individual seed passes. Within us is the embryo of the Image of God, however sullied and disfigured it may be. If given life, the Image of God will grow into the Likeness of Christ. But first, the seed must be buried in the darkness where it remains until water and warmth are given it. That is the picture of God's providential love and care. We feel buried in darkness, but all the while, He is ministering to us, providing us with what we need for rebirth as our authentic self – a strong, useful, and productive member of His household. During this stage of germination, the old self is destroyed, and new life comes forth. In due time as God supplies our needs, we break out of the darkness and stretch toward the warmth and light of Christ. As with the seed, we become far more than we were before we were buried in the dark earth, and we grow into something beautiful and bountiful for the Kingdom of God.

Knowing that this process is necessary for truly becoming a new creation makes the time of darkness less surprising and less scary. So many of us believe in Jesus Christ, want to follow Him and grow the Kingdom, and yet, we are shocked and wounded when we enter into a period of darkness, whatever the cause, sometimes feeling as if God has abandoned us. That is not so. Even as we are buried and cannot seem to reach God through prayer or worship, He is tending to our every need in order to bring forth new life. How God ministers to each of us is seldom clear, but He does. We may be aware that He is present, and still wonder why He is unresponsive to our prayers. Our assessment of the situation is shortsighted, limited by the fact that we are the creature and He is the Creator. We are not in a position to discern what He is doing from our vantage point. But like the seed that grows and becomes a thing of beauty and fruitfulness, the Spirit of God is work, shattering the shell of the sinful nature and unleashing the life of the embryo of His Image in us. We, too, will become a creature of beauty and fruitfulness, the person we did not know ourselves to be, yet always longed to become.

Often in our lives, we go through periods of darkness, but however we interpret them, we seldom expect the hardest times of life also to be opportunities for new birth and new life. We pray that our life will be restored, and we struggle to regain control and return things to "normal." This is not unlike a baby who does not wish to be born but would forever stay in the womb. Every event in life that brings us pain, fear, and suffering is not caused by God, but every time we experience pain, fear, or suffering is an opportunity for God to show us His providential care and sufficient provision. Likewise, if we seek Christ, He does grow us and set us free. Moreover, there are times when the Spirit leads us into the dark periods of life, something done almost exclusively as a result of our own sin. He allows our sin to reach its natural conclusion – burying us in misery, humiliation, and/or pain – and the process of new birth begins. Faith and trust are what sustain us in these times. On the other side of the darkness is life – if we trust and wait on the Lord. Like the Hebrews in the desert, we want to return to what we know, but the Promised Land of Christ's life awaits us if we persevere in faith and hope.

What we need to understand is that God is in the midst of the darkness, as well as what He is doing. We may feel shattered and alone without much consolation and hope from Jesus Christ. However, that state of being shattered may actually be the breaking of the casing of sin and the beginning of the new life before us. Whenever we find ourselves sitting in darkness and apparent hopelessness, we need to be still, wait, and pray. Regardless of what we see or feel, the Spirit of God is hovering over the darkness and chaos[6] that is our life

---

[6] cf. Genesis 1:2.

at that time. The seed experience is lonely, and the darkness can feel interminable. It is not. This time will pass. Moreover, it will pass with great blessing and new life if we will allow God to work in us according to His providential care. Only when we struggle and push back against the experience do we lose the value of what is happening. We do possess the freedom of will to try to stop the process and change our circumstances. If there is an obvious solution, then we need to take it. But if we decide to take a step for no reason other than movement without any clear reason except to force change, then we are thwarting the seed the experience. The process by which the old is destroyed and the new is given birth is not a matter of intellectual assent, but of experience, and everyone has to go through this process. We can fight against it, but if we do, we either prolong the experience or delay it for another time, thus losing the benefit and blessing of God would give us through this process. Obviously, the best choice is to submit to the experience, however uncomfortable and frightening it might be in the moment, allowing the Spirit to nurture and sustain us in His mysterious ways until we break forth from the darkness and stretch toward the light of Christ.

Daily Reflection and Meditation
The Seed Experience

Look back over your life and consider times of trial, be they sickness, death, broken relationships, lost jobs, or any other time of suffering and fear. What did you seek from the Lord? What was your relationship with Him at the time? Ask the Spirit to remind you of your thoughts and prayers during periods of uncertainty and fear.

_____
_____
_____
_____
_____

Can you think of a time when your life reflected the seed experience, when you felt lost and alone without God, only to discover later that He was doing a good work in you? If so, describe that time and what it has meant to your faith in Christ and your life as a disciple.

_____
_____
_____
_____
_____

How has your Father used hard and/or painful times to draw you close to Him and to change you? What was the change in you that He brought about?

_____

The Last Prayer before Death

_____

_____

_____

_____

_____

If you have not been through an experience like this, or if you did and did not recognize it as the opportunity for God to bring forth new life in you, would you trust Christ Jesus the next time you find yourself in a circumstance of seeming despair and hopelessness? Why or why not?

_____

_____

_____

_____

_____

_____

Life vs. Religion

The atrophy of Christian life and faith began with the legalization of Christianity in AD 313. That is not to say that Christianity died in the early fourth century, and what we have today is something else. Christianity is still being taught, and in times and places throughout history, Christianity has experienced revival and renewal. But death and atrophy are two different things. Death is, well, *death*. Atrophy is the weakening and deterioration of something, usually associated with a body part, and I can think of no word more apropos for the withered life of the Body of Christ than atrophy.

The Edict of Milan legalizing Christianity was issued in AD 313 by Emperor Constantine. At the time approximately one-tenth of the citizens of the Roman Empire were Christian, but Constantine ordered churches rebuilt, cash settlements paid to families left without wage earners as a result of persecution, and practiced Christianity himself, although he was not baptized until he was near death. With Constantine's conversion to Christianity came the ruling elite of the Roman Empire, some immediately and others trickling in over time. Likewise, the head of every family also brought the members of the family into the Christian faith, regardless of personal inclination or preference. Romans were baptized into Christianity *en masse* in the fourth and fifth centuries until Greco-Roman religion essentially died out and was relegated to the status of myth.[7] The problem of nominal Christianity was born, and the atrophy of the Body began.

In John 15, the Apostle reported Jesus' counsel to His disciples as follows:

> If the world hates you, keep in mind that it hated Me first. If you belonged to the world, it would love you as its own. As it is, you do not belong to the world, but I have chosen you out of the world. That is why the world hates you. Remember the words I spoke to you: 'No servant is

---

[7] Greco-Roman mythology worshiped myriad gods that reflected the best pagan explanation for the origins of creation, the realization of the divine, and the cause and effect of human behavior. The reason paganism gave way to Christianity was not solely because Constantine made it legal and converted to it, although that was a prominent factor. Christianity as it became widely known and understood was based in historical facts and events, not fantastical speculation drawn from natural phenomena. In this sense, fact trumped assumption.

greater than his master.' If they persecuted Me, they will persecute you also. If they obeyed My teaching, they will obey yours also.[8]

Once the world came into the Church, hatred and persecution ceased to be a part of the life of most Christians, although pockets of persecution continued in more remote areas. Prior to its legalization, a person had to believe the events of history and the personal meaning of those events at great risk. Christianity was not a "take it or leave it" life choice in the first three centuries of the Church's existence. To the contrary, if true, then Christianity held an irrevocable claim on the life of the believer, and the Christian worshipped a different God and lived in contrast and contradiction to the way in which everyone around him lived, thus, the isolation, persecution, and martyrdom. When everyone became Christian and "Christendom" became a geographical entity, a national and/or cultural identity (as in, peoples were defined by the geographical borders of the Church), Christianity made the transition from the birth of new creations participating in the life of God to a religion. The Christian religion maintained all of the practices, values, and habits of Christian life, except that Christianity was now a religion in the world and no longer distinct from it. From this standpoint, being Christian became a much easier following its legalization than it ever was as an outlaw faith.

Obviously, we take much more seriously that which can cost us our lives, and that applies to Christian faith as well. With the large influx of worldly authorities and the acceptance of Christian belief with them, being a Christian was no longer dangerous and, therefore, no longer necessarily demanding or all-consuming. One could be a Christian and go merrily along the way without any significant disruption of a thoroughly worldly life.[9]

In fact, contemporary western Christianity exemplifies this transition of Christian life into Christian belief. Today, we read the biblical stories in the

---

[8] John 15:18-20.

[9] I want to make clear that the Church always has people of great faith within it. There are individuals throughout history who bore powerful witness to the reality of God and the life and work to which He calls His children. What changed, however, is that *everyone* did not live Christian life with such intensity and conviction because it was not necessary. When Christianity was an outlaw faith, it had to be a faith of such trans-forming power and indescribable love that one was willing to die for it. That is a far cry from an easily adapted set of beliefs to a fully worldly life.

context of history, but the Christ in the stories is not the Christ of our lives. The last thing we anticipate is any form of conflict between our faith and the world in which we live, at least not at the core of our being. Moreover, we want Christian faith to be victorious in and for our world. We live in a worldly Christianity we inherited, seeking God's blessing, both in our religious and private endeavors, because we have been taught to believe that is all there is. That belief is wrong, as in, not true. We may *live* as if it is true, but we are wrong. Hopefully, by now we understand that there is much more to Christian life and faith. Precisely because it is more than worldly life, Christianity still stands in opposition to the world, still exists in the outpouring of God's Spirit into our world to bring us into union with Him, and still calls Christian believers - indeed, all the world - to abundant life. Christianity is not finally a religion in the sense that it mediates between the divine and the human. Christianity is life, specifically the Divine Life of God that draws us into union with Him and life in His Kingdom.

Daily Reflection and Meditation

Life vs. Religion

What is the difference between Christian life and the Christian religion?
_____
_____
_____
_____
_____
_____

How does the transition from Christianity as religion to Christianity as life affect your understanding and living as a disciple of Jesus Christ?
_____
_____
_____
_____
_____
_____

In what ways do you see the western church adapted to our culture?
_____
_____
_____
_____
_____

How would the church have to change if it truly were counter-cultural – an alternative to the culture in which we live?

How can and/or does the church function in our society as a reflection of the life of Christ and the Kingdom of God?

Be in prayer about the ways in which your Christianity is an easy religion in contrast to abundant life of Christ that challenges a dying world. What are ways in which your Christian belief is adapted to cultural norms rather than traditional biblical norms for human behavior?

The Last Prayer before Death

The Last Question before Death

The great glory, hope, and promise of Christianity is the Resurrection, but before Jesus got to the Resurrection, He had to pass through death. So must we. Jesus was very clear about this. "For whoever wants to save his life will lose it, but whoever loses his life for Me will find it." (Matthew 16:25) "Then He called the crowd to Him along with His disciples and said: "If anyone would come after Me, he must deny himself and take up his cross and follow Me." (Mark 8.34) "Do not suppose that I have come to bring peace to the earth. I did not come to bring peace, but a sword. For I have come to turn 'a man against his father, a daughter against her mother, a daughter-in-law against her mother-in-law - a man's enemies will be the members of his own household.'" (Matthew 10:34-36) "In the same way, any of you who does not give up everything he has cannot be My disciple." (Luke 14:33) None of us is going to be asked to die on a cross for the forgiveness of the sins of the world, but each of us will be asked to die to self. This is far harder than we expect it to be because we believe in a God of grace and mercy, not a God of suffering. But God is not causing our suffering or pain in sacrificing ourselves. Our suffering, disappointment, pain, and grief are brought on by our attachment to this world, to the comforts of the life we have, and to the control we expect to maintain over our future and our destiny. As surely as God wants to give us life, He knows we must let go of this world before we can participate in His Kingdom.

Everything we have read, discussed, prayed about, and opened our lives to comes down to the last prayer before death.

> Then Jesus went with His disciples to a place called Gethsemane, and He said to them, "Sit here while I go over there and pray." He took Peter and the two sons of Zebedee along with Him, and He began to be sorrowful and troubled. Then He said to them, "My soul is overwhelmed with sorrow to the point of death. Stay here and keep watch with Me."
>
> Going a little farther, He fell with His face to the ground and prayed, "My Father, if it is possible, may this cup be taken from Me. Yet not as I will, but as You will."

The Last Prayer before Death

Then He returned to His disciples and found them sleeping. "Could you men not keep watch with Me for one hour?" He asked Peter. "Watch and pray so that you will not fall into temptation. The spirit is willing, but the body is weak."

He went away a second time and prayed, "My Father, if it is not possible for this cup to be taken away unless I drink it, may Your will be done."

When He came back, He again found them sleeping, because their eyes were heavy. So He left them and went away once more and prayed the third time, saying the same thing.[10]

"Not my will, Father, but Your will be done." That is the prayer that leads to life, but it is the life that we receive when first we pass through the death of our will - our plans and dreams, our priorities and values, and most of all, the release of our control over our lives and our choices. We want to be filled with the Holy Spirit, and we truly want to serve the Kingdom of God. We want people to come to Christ, and we want to make a difference in our world by bringing the life and light of Christ into the darkness and death of our world. But, letting go of our life for God's freedom to use as He sees fit is the hardest thing we will ever do. Even Jesus asked for another option from His Father, some other way to accomplish God's purpose without His own full sacrifice. In fact, He practically pleaded to avoid the sacrifice of His own life to His Father's will. Yet, Jesus submitted to death on the Cross to fulfill His Father's plans. Jesus' obedience even to death led Him to the Resurrection and made possible humanity's participation in the life of God. As was true for Jesus Christ, we also cannot offer life to a decaying and dying world, unless we first have passed through death ourselves.

At some point we have to come to understand that what we have is nothing by comparison to what God gives. To know God, to be in conversation with Him, to touch eternity and taste the great banquet, to draw life from the river of life coming from the throne of the Holy Trinity, these beckon us toward our true destiny. *There* is where we belong, in our Father's Kingdom, not here where sin and evil destroy. It is a story that, if truly believed, is almost too good to believe. All that is our Father's is given to us, mysteries beyond

---

[10] Matthew 26:36-44.

anything we imagine, eternity greater than we conceive, and life... life unlike anything we know. How can we compare resuscitation with resurrection? One cheats death but only momentarily. The other is too glorious and wondrous for our minds to grasp, much less our words to describe. We think it is terrifying to let go of our world and trust there is an unknown eternal and divine life just waiting to be shared with us. But we are not the first to pass this way, and Jesus took the journey before us and more completely than anyone else ever will or ever needed to do. This life of the Trinity that is freely given to us is more desirable than anything on earth that we might attain. Jesus described it as 'a merchant of pearls who found the one of great value, then sold all he had to get the pearl.'[11] We were created for this: to know God and to worship and enjoy Him forever. Here is the answer to the insatiable longing of our being. But to receive what God wants to give us, the very thing for which we yearn and were created, we must sell all we have, give up everything, and pass through death. The way in which that happens in each of us is when we pray the prayer that Jesus prayed, "Not my will, Father, but Your will be done."

Why emphasize this so much? Because the reality is so difficult and scary... It is important to recognize our fears what they are – sinful – and to know that God is trustworthy and will see us through. Believing that the life God offers is better and worth more than the life we enjoy, or even the life we suffer, sounds great theoretically, but submitting our will to His, giving up our whole selves, and when the time comes, passing through death is a dark and lonely trek. We may well pray the prayer that leads to our spiritual, psychological, and intellectual death long before the time comes. Or, like Jesus Christ, we may pray the prayer even as we are looking that death in the face. Of one thing, we can be almost certain: we will ask the question, "Is there another way?" That is the point of this chapter. The Lord Himself did not want to pass through death and sought another way. There is not something sinful about wishing not to suffer through the death of this life, our ego, and self-determination. Yet, if we want to live, we must die, but our death is to death itself.

It seems unfair to come into a relationship with Jesus Christ, be full of enthusiasm and excitement, and to run headlong into the frightful darkness of

---

[11] cf. Matthew 13:45-46.

dying to self without any warning that the Christian death is painful. This is your warning. If you have not already started sacrificing this world for the purpose of participating in God's eternal Kingdom – be it time, priorities, income, plans, or something other – eventually you will have to do so, and that sacrifice is painful and scary. We need to understand this so we will be able to release ourselves into the arms of our Father trusting He will carry us through. Jesus does not die alone. His atonement was for all people, but to participate in His life, we too must die to this one. Knowing that theoretically is far easier than going through the death to self experientially. Wanting another easier way is not wrong or sinful. Jesus Himself wanted some other way. What is at stake is complete and total trust and dependence upon our Father, and the only means by which we ever fully trust Him is when everything is at stake, that is, life itself. How can that not be terrifying?

In the temptation of Jesus, Satan offered Jesus all the kingdoms of the earth, with all power and riches therein.[12] The thing about it is, all that Satan offered belonged to Jesus already. He had not received His fully glory and authority because He had not been crucified and Resurrected. However, the world and all that is in it belonged to Him as God the Son. The same thing is true for us as well. Our Father knows our needs,[13] and He is able to provide.[14]

Throughout our journey with Christ, we will be called to die to self because the depth and complexity of the sinful nature are never completely eradicated this side of our Father's Kingdom. The first time is the hardest. We are faced with some situation in which all of our inclinations aim us in one direction, but the call of Christ and the urging of the Spirit push us in a different direction. At this precipice, we either turn back toward the world from which we came, or we take the step that seems to drop us off a cliff. The Hebrews' dilemma becomes our own: if God does not part the waters, we will be destroyed by the Egyptians. Either Christ will catch us, or we will fail completely. That is what death to self looks like, at least the first time. What we will discover is the absolute and unfailing faithfulness of God and His abundant provision for the

---

[12] See Luke 4:5-8.
[13] cf. Matthew 6:8.
[14] See Ephesians 1:18-21 and Philippians 4:19.

journey in which He leads. All of this process begins with the last prayer before death, the prayer that Jesus Himself prayed, "Not My will, but Yours…"

Daily Meditation and Reflection

The Last Question before Death

Have you truly prayed that God will take your life and use it for His purposes, not your own? If so, how has that prayer changed the course of your life?

_____

_____

_____

_____

_____

_____

If the course of your life has not changed, if you are not being called to risk yourself for the sake of the Jesus Christ, then did you truly offer your life to Christ to use as He will? Explain your answer.

_____

_____

_____

_____

_____

_____

Ask the Holy Spirit to help you see your life in the context of God's purposes, and ask Him to reveal to you how seriously you consider discipleship, as well as your willingness to allow God's plans to become your plans.

_____

_____

_____

God's ways are not our ways. He will ask us to take the counterintuitive step, the direction that seems unlikely, even impossible. Are you ready? Ask the Spirit to prepare your heart and mind for ever-deepening faithfulness and service to the Kingdom of God. Can you do that? Why or why not?

II

Growing Up in Salvation

It was He who gave some to be apostles, some to be prophets, some to be evangelists, and some to be pastors and teachers, to prepare God's people for works of service, so that the body of Christ may be built up until we all reach unity in the faith and in the knowledge of the Son of God and become mature, attaining to the whole measure of the fullness of Christ. Then we will no longer be infants, tossed back and forth by the waves, and blown here and there by every wind of teaching and by the cunning and craftiness of men in their deceitful scheming. Instead, speaking the truth in love, we will in all things grow up into Him who is the Head, that is, Christ. From Him the whole body, joined and held together by every supporting ligament, grows and builds itself up in love, as each part does its work.

Ephesians 4:11-16

What Does That Mean?

The difference between an infant and an adult is enormous. A newborn must go through untold numbers of steps and stages including far more than physical growth before she becomes an adult. Christian life should be no different, although most of us have no idea what a mature Christian is supposed to look like, much less the steps involved in becoming one. That is not to say we do not try. To the contrary, many Christians make all sorts of efforts to be better Christians without any clear means of deciding whether we are successful in any significant degree. Part of the reason growth in Christian discipleship is an obscure pathway is precisely because the church itself is not clear about what constitutes a mature disciple. Indeed, even outlining the meaning of "growing up in salvation" was a painstaking struggle. And yet, if we grow and mature as mortals, then surely, we must recognize that growth and maturation as a child of God necessarily must occur also. So, what does it mean to grow up in our salvation?

When posed the question, "How do you measure spiritual growth in your congregation?" a young pastor gave three tangible indicators of spiritual growth in a believer. They were as follows: attendance – meaning attendance in worship, study – small group participation, and serving – involvement in missions, giving or tithing, accepting leadership roles in the church. Truth be told, these are about as strong a measurement of spiritual growth as the church can identify, and certainly, it is true that a person who is growing in his faith will do these things. However, as any pastor knows, there are a great many people in a congregation who also do these things and yet would be difficult to describe as mature Christians. One woman in a congregation I served sat on every committee, gave generously to the church, involved herself in as many forms of service as were available to her, both within and without the church, and was one of the most condescending, judgmental people I have ever known. Following a meeting of some study, I remember telling my secretary that, "If I had to be a Christian as she is a Christian, I'd just rather not be one." Sadly, she is not an isolated individual in the life of the church. Every church has too many such people among the congregation.

In some sense, therefore, we can say what a mature Christian is not: condescending, judgmental, and/or condemning. But what is a mature Christian, and what does it mean to grow up in our salvation?

To be Christian is to be like Christ. A mature Christian, then, would be a lens through which the world can see Jesus Christ. Growth could be measured primarily by the extent to which Christ is visibly present in the person. That would include external measures like worship attendance, giving, and serving, but those cannot be the primary measure. Anyone can go to worship, give money, or serve on a committee. Corporations with no religious, much less Christian, identity are regularly involved in philanthropic work locally and internationally. Thus, measuring maturation is tricky business. If being Christian is to be like Christ, then a maturing Christian will increasingly reveal Christ in his character. Jesus Christ's primary mission was to do the will of His Father, and, therefore, so is that the mission of every disciple: to do the will of our Father. Broadly defined, the will of the Father can be taken from Paul's first letter to Timothy: "This is good, and pleases God our Savior, who wants all men to be saved and to come to a knowledge of the truth. For there is one God and one Mediator between God and men, the Man Christ Jesus, who gave

Himself as a ransom for all men – the testimony given in its proper time."[1] But there is more. We are to do the will of our Father with the heart and mind of Christ Himself. We are actually to be *like* Him, to be christs in the world as He is the Christ of the world.

My first observation based upon the Ephesians passage above and the passage from 1 Timothy is that the critical foundation for growth in Jesus Christ is knowing the truth. Before we can speak the truth, we must know it. Ultimately, truth is not a particular body of doctrine, but a Person, Jesus Christ, Who identified Himself as *the* Truth.[2] In an ethos and generation of pluralism and relativism, the conviction of truth is counter-cultural and ostracizing. Yet, one cannot grow in the likeness of Christ apart from the truth. Truth is the starting point, specifically, the Truth about God revealed in Jesus Christ. To attempt to "define" the revelation of the truth about God, I refer to the following two passages.

> For God so loved the world that He gave His one and only Son, that whoever believes in Him shall not perish but have eternal life. For God did not send His Son into the world to condemn the world, but to save the world through Him.[3]

and...

> The Spirit of the Lord is on Me, because He has anointed Me to preach good news to the poor. He has sent Me to proclaim freedom for the prisoners and recovery of sight for the blind, to release the oppressed, to proclaim the year of the Lord's favor.[4]

The more that one grows in the likeness of Christ, the more will one's life be aligned with the passages above. Those qualities – qualities of a mature disciple – are: loving the world enough to go into it for its salvation, giving of self for the salvation and redemption of others without condemning people in their sin, sharing the good news to the poor, setting prisoners free, restoring sight to the blind, releasing the oppressed, and proclaiming the Lord's favor.

---

[1] 1 Timothy 2:3-6.
[2] cf. John 14:6.
[3] John 3:16-17.
[4] Luke 4:18-19.

Our ability to fulfill the purpose of Christ in the Luke passage depends upon having the heart of God for the world described in the John passage. Until such time as we love the world, however great the sin and confusion we see in it, we cannot possibly be in ministry to the world in the sense that Jesus Christ knew Himself to be in ministry and knew was His purpose. In other words, our hearts must be broken for the brokenness of the world, the woundedness of the people, and above all else, we must be filled with passion for the people of the world. That is Who God is, and, therefore, that is who we become when we grow up in our salvation.

The challenge of this description of Christian maturation is that it is virtually impossible to measure. However, we do recognize such qualities in certain individuals, and, likewise, the description at least gives us some sort of goal toward which we can strive, although all of our striving can be done only in fellowship with and as a student of the Holy Spirit.

Daily Reflection and Meditation

What Does That Mean?

How would you describe a mature Christian?

_____
_____
_____
_____
_____
_____

In what ways has the Spirit of God worked in you to grow you in Jesus Christ?

_____
_____
_____
_____
_____
_____

How do you measure your maturity as a Christian?

_____
_____
_____
_____
_____
_____

In what ways are you more like Christ than you were in the past? In what areas of your life do you not resemble Christ?

_____
_____
_____
_____
_____

Do you think knowing the truth is important to being Christian? Why or why not?

_____
_____
_____
_____
_____

The Fruit of the Spirit

Only by the indwelling of the Holy Spirit are any of us able to reflect Jesus Christ in any meaningful degree. Any other attempt to be like Christ necessarily would be confined to our own efforts and works, and while we may do more good than not, we cannot have the heart and mind of Christ unless He shares Himself with us through His Holy Spirit. Paul defined the fruit of the Spirit as "love, joy, peace, patience, kindness, goodness, faithfulness, gentleness and self-control."[5] The Holy Spirit is Christ's Spirit, and thus, these are the qualities of Jesus Christ, qualities sown in us over time as we submit to the work of the Spirit in us and are changed by Him. Moreover, these qualities are exhibited in the works we then do, the works listed above in the passage from Luke that describe the salvation, healing, and redemption of humanity. In a mature Christian, our doing flows from our being, whereas the reverse would be true of an immature Christian – doing the works of Christ without being like Christ. When we attempt to do God's work without the heart of God, we become Pharisees in spirit and demeanor.

In order to be filled with the Spirit of God, we have to be less filled with ourselves. The process of Christian maturation is a movement from selfish to selfless because that is Who Jesus Christ is: selfless in His giving and His loving. Selfless in Christianity does not mean that we cease to be as an individual, but rather, that we empty ourselves in order to be filled with love for others. In Paul's letter to the Philippians, he wrote, "Your attitude should be the same as that of Christ Jesus: Who, being in very nature God, did not consider equality with God something to be grasped, but made Himself nothing, taking the very nature of a Servant, being made in human likeness. And being found in appearance as a Man, He humbled Himself and became obedient to death – even death on a cross!"[6] The Son of God – Light from Light, True God of True God – emptied Himself to accept humanity. In response to His Self-giving, He is asking that we empty ourselves of our humanity, our pride and ego, in order to receive the divinity of the Holy Spirit. Only blind sin can explain the pride of self and create such a fear in us that we prefer selfish humanity to selfless divinity through the indwelling of the Spirit.

---

[5] Galatians 5:22b-23a.
[6] Philippians 2:5-8.

In the immediately preceding verses of Philippians, Paul pleads with the church, "If you have any encouragement from being united with Christ, if any comfort from His love, if any fellowship with the Spirit, if any tenderness and compassion, then make my joy complete by being like-minded, having the same love, being one in spirit and purpose. Do nothing out of selfish ambition or vain conceit, but in humility consider others better than yourselves. Each of you should look not only to your own interests, but also to the interests of others." This is the hardest thing for us: to empty ourselves, die to self, and in all humility to love as Christ Jesus loves us.

Recently, I have taken to praying for people who irritate me. I pray not because I am like Christ. To the contrary, I am praying because I am precisely the opposite. My prayer is not that God might fix them, but rather, that God might bless them in equal or greater proportion to my judgment. It appears after years of Christian discipleship that I possess no humility at all. Judgment of others, merited by human standards or not, is the root source of irritation with other people, and judgment is not our place. Only God is in a position to judge. In a conversation on this exact failure with a friend and colleague, he confessed his wish, "If only I could get rid of the plague of *me*..." Exactly. If only I could possess a love for others approximating my own self-love, then at last I would be moving toward freedom in Jesus Christ, being released from the terrible burden of pride, vanity, and *me*. To wake in the morning and to think not, "What do I want to do today?" or "What must I accomplish today?" would be freedom from the "plague of me" as my friend so perfectly identified our problem. Rather, what if we awoke and our first thoughts were, "Where, O Lord, would You send me today?" and "Who might I love for You today?" To live authentically in such a manner would open our hearts and minds to the fullness of God's abundant life.

Our first reaction is, "But what about me and the things I need to do or things I enjoy?" The question itself is the revelation of the selfish nature of human beings. Does God not know that we must earn a living? But if we have our being in Him, then our doing – our earning a living or tending to the business of daily life – would become a continual act of self-giving as we love each person we encountered, considering their needs more than our own, and emptying ourselves for them. But our watches, our bank statements, our satisfaction, the importance of what we have to do, all combine to feed the persistent "plague of me."

Anyone who has ever wiped the tears from the face of child knows the pure pleasure of turning sadness and fear into joy and hope, the deep delight of bringing healing. To love as Christ loves is to do the same thing in exponential ways in the lives of broken-hearted people, lives riddled with sin, haunted by defeats, littered by wrong choices, and bleeding from multiple wounds, many of which are self-inflicted. The reason such a life is so meaningful is because, "we are God's workmanship, created in Christ Jesus to do good works, which God prepared in advance for us to do."[7] No day is better spent than in being the vessel of Christ's compassion, mercy, wisdom, and love to a dark, broken, and lonely world. Being selfless in Jesus Christ does not destroy who we are as an individual. To the contrary, as we empty ourselves and are filled with the Spirit, we become more human and more alive than we can possibly be without God. We will not reach the end of life and remember the great joys of satisfying ourselves. When time in this life is drawing to a close, our best memories will be of those to whom Jesus Christ led us to love and whose lives were changed by the work of the Spirit in and through us.

---

[7] Ephesians 2:10.

Daily Reflection and Meditation
The Fruit of the Spirit

Ask Christ to show you ways in which the fruit of the Spirit is being grown in you. Describe the work of the Spirit in your life.

_____

_____

_____

_____

_____

How do you feel about 'making yourself nothing and taking on the nature of a servant?' What is your response to the idea that this has to be your goal if you are to be like Christ?

_____

_____

_____

_____

_____

In your relationships with others, how often do you strive to think of others as better than yourself? How important is it to you to look out for the interests of others as much as you look out for your own interests?

_____

_____

_____

_____

In what ways do you suffer from the "plague of me?" Should we even think of the demands of our lives and our interests as the "plague of me?" Why or why not?

Faith and Hope

When Jesus said, "you are the salt of the earth" and "you are the light of the world,"[8] I am not convinced He was referring solely or even primarily to our works. All of human life will be marked by sin, sorrow, failure, disease, death, and evil. Human life contains great blessing and happiness, but for the most part, we invest our lives in trying to survive the bad unscathed, or minimally so, longing for the good days to come again. I believe what truly constitutes the life of the world is Christ Himself, and to the extent that we bring Him into the world, then life and light overcome death and darkness. Yes, there are works we can do, indeed must do, but what matters more than the works we do is *how* we do them. The capacity to bring the sacred into the profane with grace and tenderness is the great privilege of being truly like Jesus Christ. One has only to think of how Jesus treated people – the Samaritan woman at the well,[9] the Roman centurion whose servant was sick,[10] the hemorrhaging woman,[11] the ten lepers,[12] the widow of Nain,[13] and so many more – to realize that what He brought was more than the momentary action He took. He restored life. He spread hope. And He loved.

In Paul's first letter to the church in Corinth, he describes several gifts of the Holy Spirit,[14] emphasizing the importance of love, concluding, "These three remain: faith, hope, and love. But the greatest of these is love."[15] Our world is dying for lack of faith, hope, and love. Moreover, the faith, hope, and love about which Paul speaks are divine gifts of the Holy Spirit – faith, hope, and love that are received from the heart of God then spilled into the world from our own hearts.

In our generation there is so little faith that life has any more meaning than what can be derived from work or pleasure. In short enough time, we each will be another faceless and nameless mortal forgotten in the bins of history.

---

[8] Matthew 5:13 and 14, respectively.
[9] John 4:4-26.
[10] Matthew 8:5-12.
[11] Luke 8:43-48.
[12] Luke 17:11-14. Nine of the ten lepers cured never thanked God for their healing.
[13] Luke 7:11-15.
[14] 1 Corinthians 13.
[15] Verse 13.

Growing Up in Salvation

Instinctively, we know this. Our grandparents and great-grandparents are often known only through aged photographs with their memory remaining in the telling of family stories. In due time, we too will fade away. But faith… "Now faith is being sure of what we hope for and certain of what we do not see."[16] Faith applies to far more in life than our ultimate destiny as children of God. Faith is knowing that, in spite of what we see or feel, this moment has meaning and importance because we are God's children. Faith is the deep and abiding trust that life is a gift from a generous and loving Father and therefore worth the living. Faith is the certainty that we matter and that our God knows our name and is able to sustain us regardless of what happens. Even more, faith is the firm conviction that our God will find a way to bring joy from sorrow, and laughter from tears *because* He loves us with an everlasting love. All around us people live desperate lives unaware of the strength and blessing of faith. To be able to open another's eyes to the light of faith is truly a gift of the Spirit. Faith in Jesus Christ forever transforms a life as it shatters loneliness and tears down walls of fear.

If we think about it, for what does our world hope? What is it that we as people living in the twenty-first century long to see or experience? World peace? An end to global warming? Maybe something on a smaller scale…. Security? Wealth? Beauty? The hope that is the gift of the Holy Spirit gives buoyancy and courage to everyday life. Yes, we hope for eternity. We should long for the time when finally we will meet our Father face to face. That hope is the greatest of hopes, for it keeps us afloat when life threatens to overwhelm us. But hope in Christ also stretches into every area of life – that the power of sin will one day be broken, that our fears do not the measure the future, that our broken relationships can be restored, that our deepest wounds can be healed. Hope lifts us beyond the cages to which we are accustomed and sets us free. Being full of hope is not being an unrealistic optimist. To the contrary, Christian hope reveals itself most clearly when in times of darkness and trouble. True hope is born of the power of God's victory in Jesus Christ. Nothing we face will ever be greater than God's ability and willingness to overcome. It is precisely our hope in Jesus Christ that allows us to hope for our world and to speak hope into the lives of those who despair. Hope is a light, a yearning, a confidence that good is yet to come and the best awaits us still.

---

[16] Hebrews 11:1.

When we hope only for this world, we are, as Paul says, to be pitied the most.[17] It is the hope of eternity that gives substance to our hopes for the world, not vice versa.

In his letter to the church in Rome, Paul wrote, "we rejoice in the hope of the glory of God. Not only so, but we also rejoice in our sufferings, because we know that suffering produces perseverance; perseverance, character; and character, hope. And hope does not disappoint us, because God has poured out His love into our hearts by the Holy Spirit, whom He has given us."[18] The reason Paul can say he rejoices in suffering – as we perhaps can as well someday – is because his suffering had been tried. He persevered and did not give up on God. In the course of his life, his perseverance gave way to character as he learned, grew, and matured in faith, until his character became certain hope in Christ. This is the progression of growth in our salvation. We cannot give up the first time we suffer, regardless of the reason we suffer. Life will bring suffering one way or the other, and if we persevere in faith, our character grows. We become stronger. Eventually our hope in Christ is satisfied by the love He pours out into our lives. Our hope is never denied, not even in death. This sort of hope brings a steadiness to our world, a calm in the middle of the whirlwind of life around us. It is the gentle but unfailing optimism founded on God's faithfulness, not in our planning and doing. Yes, we should hope for things in this world, but the hope that lifts hearts and springs anew throughout our lives is the hope that the Spirit gives us, a divine and holy hope in the goodness and providence of God.

---

[17] cf. 1 Corinthians 15:19.
[18] Romans 5:2b-5.

Daily Reflection and Meditation

Faith and Hope

Why do you want to be a Christian?

_____
_____
_____
_____
_____
_____

What difference does the faith of Christians make in our world? More specifically, how does your faith in Jesus Christ impact the people around you?

_____
_____
_____
_____
_____
_____

Describe the hope in your own life. How is your hope conveyed to those around you?

_____
_____
_____
_____
_____
_____

FROM GLORY INTO GLORY

How is perseverance to character and character to hope real in you? Is the love of God the focus of your hope? If so, how?

_____
_____
_____
_____
_____
_____

And the Greatest Is Love

Peter wrote, "Above all, love each other deeply, because love covers over a multitude of sins."[19] Our world aches for love, not facile affection or lust, but truly to be loved. Genesis tells the story of creation including the distinctive creation of man and woman and ends with the statement, "The man and his wife were both naked, and they felt no shame."[20] To be naked and unashamed is to be fully known and fully loved. Ultimately, only God knows us fully and loves us perfectly, but every human being yearns to be both known and loved. Our society expresses love in myriad forms of beauty or perversion, but all forms are the expression of the greatest longing of every human heart. What each person's soul cries is, "if you truly know me as I am, can you love me?" And the answer for most of us is no. For this reason we hide behind pretenses and defenses, often subconsciously, guarding ourselves against our own unlovability. But love is a gift of the Spirit, and like a warm blanket on a cold night, godly love sees and still covers the sins of others. Godly love protects people from the rejection we sense should come because of who we really are. It is the healing balm for every human soul, and it is the most powerful tool of transformation that exists. Selfless love beckons people to live and to be free. We are drawn to those who love unreservedly without even understanding why we are. If a Christian can do anything for Jesus Christ, he can love others. One does not have to be talented or smart or skilled or healthy to love the world with the love that God has poured into the hearts of His children.

In his first letter the Apostle John wrote, "We know that we live in Him and He in us, because He has given us of His Spirit. And we have seen and testify that the Father has sent His Son to be the Savior of the world. If anyone acknowledges that Jesus is the Son of God, God lives in him and he in God. And so we know and rely on the love God has for us. God is love. Whoever lives in love lives in God, and God in him."[21] Having been born of the Spirit and living in God, we are new creations. Our confession of faith is in Jesus Christ, the Son of God and Savior of the world. Coming to live as a child of God and accepting the identity of Christian faith are the foundations of new life in Christ. When we begin to know with certainty that God's love is

---

[19] 1 Peter 4:8.
[20] Genesis 2:25.
[21] 1 John 4:13-16.

trustworthy and reliable, that He will not fail us, we have begun to mature as a Christian. Enough separation between ourselves and the world exists that our faith and hope depend upon God more than the world. Yet, maturity in Christian life manifests itself in love. Not only do we rely on the love of God for us, but we begin to live out of that love. When divine love – love received from God – begins to seep into the essence of who we are, we are growing up in our salvation and becoming more like Jesus Christ.

The chief characteristic God has revealed to us of Himself is love. From Genesis to Revelation, the Bible reveals the passionate, holy, relentless love story between God and His people, first the Jews, then all peoples and nations. That love remains the primary force driving God's desire to save and redeem the whole and every individual therein. The breadth, depth, and determination of the love of God is so great that the Apostle John went so far as to identify God as love itself.[22] Thus, the defining characteristic of a mature Christian must also be love – a heart broken for others and a passion to reach them and draw them into the love of Christ for them. In the Gospel according to John, Jesus said, "By this all men will know that you are My disciples, if you love one another."[23] What identifies a disciple of Jesus Christ is love. Living in the Truth that is Jesus Christ demands that we grow from our innate selfishness until we are filled with the selfless love of God for His world. "For God so *loved* the world…"[24] This world, our world, is the world God loves. Every generation is a new generation of people whom God loves: sinful people, mean people, fearful people, confused and lost people, every kind of people in every mode of existence. This is the generation into which we are born, and this generation of people is the one given us to love as Christ loves.

Being the salt of the earth and light of the world refers to far more than our actions. It encompasses the being we bring to our actions. That which pushes back the encroaching darkness around us is not the works we do, but rather the faith, hope, and love with which we do anything and everything. It is the presence of a different type of humanity, the humanity that was seen in Jesus Christ that brings transformation to the world. In this way, by the life and power of the Holy Spirit in us, Christ is ever-present in each new generation.

---

[22] cf. 1 John 4:7.
[23] John 13:35.
[24] John 3:16a, *emphasis added*.

He is, however, constrained by our willingness to grow up in our salvation and by our desire to be healed of the "plague of me." When Christians do not mature in Christ, the darkness of sin and evil grows in the world. Only as we commit to growing up in our salvation is God given free rein to love the world through us and to bring the life-giving transformation of faith, hope, and love.

Daily Reflection and Meditation
And the Greatest Is Love

When you imagine yourself to be most Christian, what do you envision?

_____
_____
_____
_____
_____

How often do you pray to be filled with love for others that is as unconditional as God's love for you?

_____
_____
_____
_____
_____

Where do you see the self-giving love of God in you that was not there earlier in your life? In what ways do you love more from the abundance of God's love than you once did?

_____
_____
_____
_____
_____

How well is the "plague of me" quenched by love for others in you?

Christian love is actually a gift of the Holy Spirit. Has the Spirit poured out the love of Christ in your heart, and if so, how?

The State of the Church

The church today needs mature Christians. That has been true of every generation, but it is especially true today. Some years ago in seminary, I took a year-long class in the history of Christian doctrine. *Doctrine* is nothing more, and nothing less, than the contours of what we believe to be true. The course began with the formation of the canon of Scripture followed by the development of Christian doctrine – the authoritative teaching of the Christian Church for the salvation of the world. During the year of study, we moved steadily forward through the centuries eventually arriving at contemporary Christian doctrine, such as it is. Although generally settled within decades of Jesus' life, death and Resurrection, in the first two- to three-hundred years of Christianity, the canon of Scripture and Christian doctrine were gathered and officially established as the treasures of the revelation of our salvation, indeed, of the salvation and redemption of the whole of creation. In contrast, the most recent two- to three-hundred years have witnessed the reversal of that process: we have seen the *de*formation of Christian revelation, first in the substance of Christian teaching – doctrine – and finally, in the deconstruction of Holy Scripture. Whereas, historically, theology[25] reigned as the highest form of thought, during and following the Enlightenment and the age of reason, theology became subservient to fashionable schools of philosophy. As a result, the revelation of the God in Jesus Christ more and more reflected human thought and was interpreted and reinterpreted by each new idea that sprang from the minds of men and women. Christianity as a religion has become a smorgasbord of disjointed beliefs, and the universal Christian Church is

---

[25] The literal meaning of the word *theology* originates out of the Greek language and means reasoned talk about or wisdom about God. Because "god" in every civilization and expression incorporates the origins, purpose, meaning, and destiny of humanity, theology necessarily was held to be the highest form of human thought. Thomas Aquinas called theology the divine science. Modern philosophy and science, even in abandonment of the Judeo-Christian God, seek to become the supreme theology of the day by discerning the origins, purpose, meaning, and destiny of human beings. Most theories simply do so without reference to God, but the goal is the same, the distinction being that human philosophical and scientific explanations are the product of human construct, whereas true theology is received. Christian theology is the elucidation of God's Self-revelation and as the Creator, thus, the added revelation of who we are, from where we came, why we are here, and to where we are headed.

fractured and disunited into various schools of interpretation and teaching. In short, we have become the church Paul warned against "tossed back and forth by the waves, and blown here and there by every wind of teaching…"

What we believe and what we teach impacts greatly who Christians are and what the Church becomes. A Christian church separated from the truth of revelation and the love of Christ given by the Holy Spirit in maturation cannot survive for it ceases to be anything more than a human construct. Things made by humans exist only as long as the humans who are the driving force remain. Moreover, there is nothing distinct or transforming or life-giving about human institutions. They rise; they fall. There is certainly no maturation in Christian life, no transition from our fallen state into Christ-like children of God bringing faith, hope, and love into our world.

The western church today is divided in multiple factions, not simply by denomination, but also within denominations. There is no clear continuity in the proclamation of the Gospel, and far too often, obvious contradictions divide our message to the world. The state of the church invites disdain in a culture already saturated with secular thought and disregard for all things sacred. Within Methodism, certainly, but also within all other mainline (now often identified as "old line") denominations, conflict and division have increased steadily through the last four or five decades. If division has not occurred outright, it is occurring quietly as people slowly bleed out the back doors and do not return.

We need to understand this time in the context of God's plans and purposes. God is working for the salvation and redemption of the world. That *is* His plan. When His people cease to be faithful, He calls them and urges them back to Him. If we stay in a state of rebellion long enough, He grants us our wishes. He allows us to go in the direction of our own choosing, and apart from God, human beings will not choose Christ's Kingdom and salvation. But always, *always*, God will call those with open hearts to Him, and He will renew His purposes through these. The Holy Spirit does not fade or wither, and where the Spirit is, there is life. Whether we identify this time period as a pruning – a cutting back of wild growth or dead branches – or the maintaining of a remnant of the faithful is less important than understanding that the years ahead are going to be hard – hard, but an amazing adventure. What this generation and beyond have the privilege of witnessing is the Spirit's renewal of the church, the work of God to recreate the church in faithfulness and obedience. He will unleash His power to give life through those who wait for Him and trust Him. Participation in the coming renewal truly will require walking by faith because so much of the church needs transformation. Both sides of the primary division around the revelation of God in Jesus Christ – made known through Scripture and the Creed – are in need of a deeper, more profound understanding of the Gospel, as well as how to go about living of the Gospel. Because we have seen God work in history, we can be certain that He is not only willing but able to renew and restore the church so that it functions as Christ's Body in the world, working for the salvation and redemption of the world. You and I cannot possibly know exactly how God will work or what will be the outcome, but we can know with absolute certainty that God will not abandon His work in the world.

The world around us is hungry, yearning, lost, and searching for meaning and substance for life and living. Quite literally, the harvest is plentiful.[26] Our world needs the faith, hope, and love that Christ will spread far and wide through willing workers. For us to become workers in the harvesting of the fields for our Father, we must grow up in our salvation and be prepared – unified in faithfulness, humble in the knowledge of God, committed to take our place in the Body of Christ, and bound together in love. It is time to accept that we are invited to be part of something far greater than our personal lives and to produce fruit that will last beyond this moment in time.

---

[26] cf. Luke 10:2.

Daily Reflection and Meditation

The State of the Church

From your experience and observation, where and how do you see disunity among contemporary Christians – tossed about by every wind of teaching?

_____
_____
_____
_____
_____

How does what you believe relate to how you live and love as a Christian?

_____
_____
_____
_____
_____

Many churches are suffocating from terminal "niceness," so much so that we conspicuously ignore deeply divisive issues among ourselves. Do you think the pretense of unity helps or harms our witness? Explain your answer.

_____
_____
_____
_____

How can your witness to the Truth that is Jesus Christ be an expression of great love for others, both on an individual level and in the corporate life of the church?

How do you intend to cope with division in the church as the Holy Spirit allows decline and brings renewal?

III

Entering the Promised Land

Seeing the God of Scripture in Our Lives

The first key to growth in Christ - growing in His image and likeness - is knowing which biblical story applies to you. Frankly, only the Spirit reveals that to you, but understanding people's actions, reactions, and responses in the Bible guides us in our own life and decisions with the help of the Holy Spirit, either to make the right choice or to correct our course. The Bible is the account of God's actions in history, particularly the extended history with His people in the Old Testament. Using the book of Joshua, we will revisit the Israelites move into the Promised Land, the land of Canaan.

Often, when we read the stories of the Bible, they seem like a curiosity, an account of something that happened a very long time ago. While the biblical stories may be interesting, they do not seem immediately relevant or applicable to our lives. That is especially true of the Old Testament where accounts tend to be off-putting in that we do not like the idea of wars and the destruction of whole cities of people. Yet, God does not change, and neither does human nature. The attitudes and behavior of human beings four thousand years ago do not differ significantly from our attitudes and behavior. Of course, in today's society, murder is bad, but murder was wrong in the Old Testament, ranking in the Big Ten that God gave Moses on Mount Sinai. Contemporarily, we cringe at the idea that God directs His people to destroy other nations, as if war is somehow more justifiable if it is ordered by a president than by God. Today we imagine God as removed from the more vile aspects of human life, such inevitabilities as war or poverty or disease. Yet, if God is anything, He is involved in His creation. Moreover, He addresses each society and culture in each epoch of history in the manner in which human beings live, not in some divine realm, unreachable and unintelligible to a fallen world.

The book of Joshua records God's instructions for entering and conquering the land of the Canaanites, land He promised to Abraham centuries before Moses, Joshua, and the Israelites arrived in the area. At a time in history when gods were measured by their military strength and ability to gain land for their people, the God of Abraham, Isaac, and Jacob responded in kind. Through Joshua, God guided the Israelites as they took possession of the land by force through war and destruction. As we shall see, there are important lessons for us in the battles that the Israelites fought; their losses, their victories, and their mistakes along the way, all teach us something about the unchanging relationship between God and His people.[1] Most of us are inclined to think of the entrance into Canaan in fairly simplistic terms: God rescued the people from slavery, led them through the desert, and gave them the Promised Land. Part of the reason we think this way is because we prefer not to think too hard about the violence and death we associate with the Old Testament history. Yet, the Israelites' entrance into the Promised Land was a long and arduous process,

---

[1] In the ancient world, wars were fought for gods and that which the gods could give them - good land, power, harvest, rain, and other necessary conditions for a people's survival. We imagine that our wars are different, but we are mistaken. If we look at recent wars in the Middle East and the threat of fundamentalist Islam to the Western world are almost exclusively about their Allah and our perceived godlessness, including what they believe to be our exploitation of their natural resources, specifically oil. Historically, the United States did go to war for humanitarian reasons most of the time, if we are fair about US history and our intervention in various national and/or international wars, although certainly, provocation and national interest brought us into the World Wars.

In contrast to accepted American foreign policy, redeemingly, George W. Bush believed in democracy and freedom for all people rather than the inevitable status quo of benevolent dictators or even oppressive dictators. Beyond that deep conviction of the president, the other reasons for entering the wars in the Middle East revolved around potential threats and our national interest in oil supply. Whether one agrees with the wars is a matter of personal opinion. My point is that nations go to war for their gods, which is the primary, though not exclusive, reason fundamentalist Islam is at war with the West, particularly the US. The US, however, went to war for the protection of the international community from aggrandized threats, as well as for the economic necessity of a stable oil supply - *which reveals something to us about our gods*. A secular society does not have gods, except for material gods such as oil and practical gods such as safety. This is why there is such deep division and acrimony in the nation regarding the wars. A secular society is not unified by any god and therefore can never be unified about any national foreign policy or standard of law and morality.

On an aside note, while I do not disagree with former-President Bush about every human being's desire for freedom, our image of freedom is secular in nature, and a democratic Islamic nation will vote for its religious convictions, including Sharia law, except to the extent that that nation takes on the values of western secularism. A religious people eventually are incompatible with a secular state.

conquering one city or tribal kingdom at a time. That is the reason we are using the book of Joshua as a tool for understanding maturation in Christian life. The conquest of the Canaanites prefigures the conquest of sin in our own lives, just as the Israelites' possession of the Promised Land does the pathway of Christian maturation.

When we become the new creation described in the first study, it is not unlike the Israelites standing east of the Jordan and looking into the land of Canaan. So much is promised to them, and they have virtually no idea how to get what is promised. We have been born of the Holy Spirit into the Kingdom of God, brothers and sisters of Christ Himself, and we haven't a clue how any of that is made real in our lives. No amount of confidence that we are a new creation in Christ Jesus translates into a mature Christian. Just as the Israelites stood at the border of the Promised Land waiting for instructions on how to possess the land that God had promised their ancestors, so also do we stand at the threshold of new life in Christ waiting for instructions on how to become fit for the Kingdom of God, an authentic, participating member of the family of God. I do not want to detract from the historical significance of the conquest of Canaan, but I do want to use the lessons learned in that conquest as examples of lessons we must learn in order to grow up in our salvation.

Daily Reflection and Meditation
Seeing the God of Scripture in Our Lives

Have you ever read a biblical story and realized it applied to your life at that time? If so, describe what was happening and your response.

_____
_____
_____
_____
_____

Can you see the same situation and circumstances in your own life in biblical accounts you read, in spite of cultural differences? Discovering ourselves in the people of Scripture is critical for Christian maturation. Describe spiritual lessons you have taken from historical events in the Bible.

_____
_____
_____
_____
_____

What stories of the Bible speak to the experiences, dilemmas, and triumphs in your life? How have those stories shaped and informed the decisions you have made?

_____
_____
_____

Entering the Promised Land

Entering the Promised Land

The book begins with the LORD reiterating His promise of the land, as well as His personal promise to be with Joshua as He was with Moses. This alone is comparable to God's promise to us: we are born into the family of God,[2] and are co-heirs with Jesus Christ[3] of our Father's Kingdom. When Joshua sent scouts to "look over the land, especially Jericho" (2:1), they met Rahab who hid them from the king and allowed the spies to escape unharmed. In return, her home and family were protected from destruction when Jericho was handed over to the Israelites. The encounter with Rahab does not easily equate with our growth in Jesus Christ. Canaan was a hostile land, and the Kingdom of God is the opposite. Before turning to Rahab, though, we should note the hostility encountered by the Israelites as they moved into the Promised Land. The Israelites experienced resistance to their move into the Promised Land, and so will we encounter antagonism to new life as brothers and sisters of Christ Jesus – not the military hostility the Israelites met, but rather, the cultural disdain for the new direction of our lives. To the extent that a congregation or denomination has become enculturated, the church itself can be hostile toward authentic discipleship.

What we can see, however, is that God provides help and assistance along the way. People will come into your life and assist you when you need it most. There is no evidence that the spies knew Rahab was friendly or supportive of Israel. Why they chose to go to the home of a prostitute is not clear, probably because she was least likely to reject them, but there is no doubt that their success in scouting out Jericho was made possible by her protection. In the same way, there are times in our life when we will find ourselves with the most unlikely of people who offer to us exactly what we need in that time or circumstance. These are people God providentially places in our pathway for the express purpose of helping us. We need to trust that, when we are stuck or lost, God will provide the guidance and help we need - not might, *will*.

Before Joshua and the Israelites could enter the Promised Land, they first had to cross the Jordan. As He did with Moses, God stopped the flow of water. As He ordered, Joshua had the priests stand in the middle of the dried Jordan

---

[2] cf. John 1:12-3.
[3] cf. Romans 8:17.

River while all of Israel crossed over. For us as Christians, Jesus Christ already has accomplished this on our behalf. That is the point of the Incarnation, Death, and Resurrection: to build a bridge between heaven and earth, a fact exponentially greater than damming the river. Still, the imagery of the Ark of the Covenant held in the middle of the Jordan making possible the passage from the forty-year desert trek into the Promised Land is a powerful sign revealing what was to come and did indeed occur in Jesus Christ. Is there any sense in which we can imagine Joshua knew the future significance of what was happening? No. But what God did in the past foreshadows what He will do in the future, and His consistency is an assurance and encouragement for us because we can trust that He will act with us as He did with everyone before us.

Another important lesson to be learned is that, though movement may seem impossible to us, God will provide a way forward. This is in fact something God wants us to understand clearly. Events and circumstances in life can lead to seemingly impossible dead-ends, but nothing is impossible for God. If we are striving to be faithful and to pursue God's purposes with our lives and in our world, God will make a way forward for us, regardless of how impossible a situation may appear to us.

The well-known story of the Fall of Jericho reveals important clues for discipleship. The Israelite military men marched around the city with the priests carrying the Ark of the Covenant. On the seventh day, the priests blew trumpets, the men shouted, and the walls collapsed. This is an obviously absurd means of conquering a city, but it is what the LORD commanded them to do. The leap of faith required to become disciples can seem equally absurd to us. Is it not enough simply to believe without having to give our whole selves to Jesus Christ? Certainly, a great many Christians believe in God but do not trust Him or have a meaningful relationship with Him. I am not endorsing such nominal Christianity, but neither am I prepared to condemn a superficial believer to hell. That is not my place, and I strongly suspect God is more merciful than I. What I can say with certainty is that the abundant life and joy Jesus promised us is not found in nominal faith. It is when we make the conscious decision to accept and own our inheritance as a child of God that we begin to experience His power and His faithfulness to us. Israel's first experience with God as they entered the Promised Land was one of spectacular victory, and so also do we often experience a spiritual "high" when we first submit to Christ.

A second important lesson is also embedded here. If we are ever to grow in Christ, we must agree to do those things the Spirit leads us to do, even if it makes no sense to us. I'm not suggesting that we become irrational or unreasonable, but God wants us to step out in faith, to learn to trust Him, so we can accomplish those things He wants us to do. God is able to convey His wishes. Although the reason for an action may be unclear to us, we will feel compelled to take a step. Approaching a Canaanite prostitute was unusual behavior at best for Israelite spies, but that unusual step proved to be their protection and salvation from death, a favor returned to Rahab by the Israelites when they attacked and conquered Shittim. In small ways, most of us already have experienced this type of phenomenon – the sudden urge to call an old friend, for example, whom we discover is in need of our friendship at exactly the moment we call. This is a prompting of the Spirit, and if we consistently follow those promptings, we quickly become more aware of when God is speaking to us versus when we are coming up with ideas and plans of our own.

Daily Reflection and Meditation
Entering the Promised Land

When were you first aware that faith is more than belief and were drawn into a relationship with Jesus Christ? (Some people have significant, datable conversions. Others slowly come into a personal relationship with Jesus Christ. The question is: when did *you* become aware…?)

_____

_____

_____

_____

_____

How did God win you?

_____

_____

_____

_____

_____

Describe a time when the providence of God was evident in your life. When and how did God provide for you and work for your good before you became aware He was doing so?

_____

_____

_____

_____

FROM GLORY INTO GLORY

Entering the Promised Land

Learning Obedience and Submission

The LORD also instructed the Israelites to take all the gold, silver, iron, and bronze and put them in the tabernacle treasury. Beyond that, the military was to destroy the entirety of Jericho, including men, women, and children, then to burn the whole city to the ground. Bear in mind how important it was at that time to establish the power of a god through military conquest. But more importantly, Jericho represented Israel's first encounter with the Canaanite religion as well as the people. Part of the significance of the destruction of everything in Jericho reveals something more than the superiority of the God of Israel. Complete destruction also meant that the Canaanite religion was not available to the Israelites. Nothing was left to tempt them. Some of the prayers and requests God refuses are for our benefit. He refuses, quite literally, so as not to lead us into temptation.

God wants to destroy idolatry in our lives, the worship of false gods, something we all do. Be it material things, human love, wealth, or even church, God wants to destroy our idols. When we consider the desolation of Jericho's remains, we catch a glimpse of what it feels like for us when God destroys our idols. We want Jesus Christ to come be with us and bless us. In contrast, Christ came that we might be raised with Him. To receive the abundant life of Christ, we first have to release the shadows of life to which we cling. Rahab recognized that the Israelite God was more powerful than her god, but no one else in Jericho appeared to arrive at the same conclusion. Similarly, a part of us really yearns for the fullness of life in Christ and wants to risk it all to receive life, but only a part. The rest of us want the comfort, security, and pleasure of the life we have now, only with God's blessing. God is not amenable to such an agreement.

Jesus said, "It is easier for a camel to go through the eye of a needle than for a rich man to enter the kingdom of God."[4] Wealth itself is not bad, but it does lend itself to a host of idols - homes, automobiles, travel, clothing, and worse, wrong inclinations of the heart and mind, sometimes not-so-hidden feelings of superiority or condescension toward others, for example. Wealth can be of great service to the Kingdom of God, but if wealth is our idol, we can be sure that, if we truly desire to be a Christian, God will begin to diminish

---

[4] Mark 10:25.

our wealth. He will not allow idols to stand between Him and us. Isolating wealth as an idol, however, is picking the low hanging fruit. We all know what Jesus said. Other forms of idolatry are less obvious, but equally dangerous for truly living in Christ. Christians are often guilty of worshiping their church or worshiping the Bible. Even more so than the inherent pitfalls of wealth, both of these are instrumental mysteries that lead us to the throne of God, but they are not God. If our love for the church or the Bible is greater than our relationship with God, He will destroy that idol as well. If Jesus' life on earth tells us anything, it tells us of the dangers of religiosity and the rule of the Book instead of the love of God. Religious idols are just as deadly as any worldly idol. Idolatry leads to death, and Christ leads to life. It's very simple, but, oh, so very painful to learn.

The next city the Israelites were to conquer was the city of Ai. Ai did not appear dangerous, so the whole army of Israel was not sent on the mission. But the men of Ai defeated the Israelite army and chased them away. Upon their return, the LORD commanded Joshua to bring the tribes together in order to discover who had kept items meant for the LORD'S treasury for themselves. Going through the clans, eventually Achan of the tribe of Judah confessed that he had taken some of the wealth from Jericho and buried it under his tent. The items were recovered, and Achan and all of his family were stoned to death before being burned.

The story is so harsh and without grace from our perspective today. But we need to realize that God hates it when we withhold a part of ourselves from Him. We say we are His servants committed to discipleship, but then we hold back that part of ourselves that we do not want to give up - some selfish desire or pet indulgence, sometimes simply out of fear. Frankly, we withhold a great deal from God, oftentimes as sins of omission. We do not fully know ourselves and our idols as God does. We cannot sacrifice to God what we do not know we are keeping. The day will come, though, when God reveals these impurities within us and wants to purge them. Letting them go feels horrible. For example, if one goes through an unwanted divorce and continues to cling to the hope of an impossible past, releasing the past with its broken heart and great disappointments is hard to do. But God is not in our past, and life is not in the past. God is in today, and He will go to great lengths to set us free from these misguided and very human attachments. The point is freedom, but we do not see that when we are enmeshed in some quagmire of life.

Following the cleansing of Israel through the death of Achan and his family, God again began to lead the Israelites forward, and Ai was destroyed. This time, the Israelites were allowed to keep the plunder, unlike God's expectation that everything be placed in the treasury. This is a glimpse of how we begin to taste abundant life. As God breaks our unhealthy attachments and attitudes, He replaces them with greater life than we thought we had. Giving up something precious to us, even a value or moral we hold dear, hurts, but in return, God gives us more. This is the process of dying to self, one step at a time. We cannot guide the process because we do know not what chain (sin) God wants to break first. He alone grows us perfectly.

Daily Reflection and Meditation
Learning Obedience and Submission

Looking back on your life, can you see times when you held onto things or situations or attitudes that were bad for you and your relationships, especially with God? Describe such a time.

_____
_____
_____
_____
_____
_____

Identify three areas of your life that you are withholding from God, even if only in the sense that you think you should be able to handle some small thing on your own without bothering God. Are the bigger parts of your life what you withhold from God? If, after honest reflection, you cannot identify three things in your life that you have not shared with God, ask the Holy Spirit to do so.

_____
_____
_____
_____
_____
_____

What are you afraid of losing by fully committing your life to Christ?

_____
_____
_____

How do you feel about God's willingness to destroy our idols, even if it hurts terribly at the time?

The Wonder and Healing of Providence

Joshua, Chapter 9, opens with the widespread concern among area kings about Israel's mighty God. Several kings came together to prepare to go to war, but the Gibeonites opted to deceive Israel by presenting themselves as a remote kingdom, and, therefore, not a threat to Israel. With this deception, they asked - and received - a peace treaty with Israel through Joshua. However, in verse 14, the Bible records that they "did not inquire of the LORD," the implication being that Joshua and his leaders were deceived because they made decisions based on their own wisdom. Three days later, the men of Israel discovered that the Gibeonites actually lived near them. Rather than break the peace treaty, they allowed the Gibeonites to live, but only as free labor for Israel. They continued to live peacefully among the Israelites, some even converting to Judaism.

Initially, this story simply reveals the providence of God at work in our lives. When we make a choice based on human wisdom, even a wrong choice that is not what God wants us to do, He will use our mistakes providentially for our own good. This is a huge gift. There is great freedom in the providence of God. When, with all sincerity and good intentions, we do the wrong thing, God adapts to our errors and works with us to bring forth good. We do not know what God would have said if the Israelite leaders had asked Him about the Gibeonites, and we will never know. Likewise, we will never know what God would have done had we chosen a different course or made a different choice. God does not entertain "what ifs" but works with "what is." If we are engaging in a discussion of "What if...?" then our conversation is not with Jesus Christ, nor is it helpful in our journey with Him. But we must admit, some "what ifs" are excruciating. "What if I had just locked the gate and my child had not wandered into the street?" That is a "what if" that can haunt a person for life. Would haunt a person for life... We will discuss how God uses these sorts of events in our lives to heal us and grow us, but regrets are sometimes horrible. When a mistake is made, by choice or unintentionally, we need to know that God will use it for good, even if we cannot imagine how at the time.

But the story does not stop there. Five Amorite kings united to attack Gibeon, whose king then called upon Joshua and the Israelites for help. True to their promise, the Israeli warriors marched through the night, arriving at

Entering the Promised Land

Gibeon at dawn and surprising the five kings and their armies. The text actually reads, "The LORD threw them into confusion before Israel, who defeated them in a great victory at Gibeon. (10:10) When Israel pursued retreating forces following their victory at Gibeon, first the LORD reigned hail on the Amorites before making the sun stand still, giving Joshua and his men time to catch and destroy all those who fled. At face value, the story is unusual at least. God made the sun to stand still? That is what is recorded in Joshua, as a response to Joshua's request for more daylight hours to catch the enemy.

What we can take from this story is greatly encouraging. When we are seeking God and desire to serve His purposes, He will fight with us and for us. We need to know that when the task before us seems too great and too hard. Likewise, when we are facing enemies within - fears, doubts, anger, wounded and broken hearts - if we try to remain steadfast on the path God has set before us, He will fight for us, fight to defeat our fear and instill trust, overcome our doubt and grow confidence in Him, and on and on. The obvious implication is that the human heart, mind, and soul are full of these forms of slavery, and growth in Christ - coming to know the truth about our God and of our salvation - continually sets us free from such basic expressions of the sinful nature. The point needs to be made, however, that this growth and this healing and freedom come while we are pursuing God's plans and purpose. If we sit at home and maintain life as usual, there is little or no cause for growth, no time or place to see God fight for us, no challenge that requires God to rescue us. We can read about these things, but we cannot *know* these truths until we are committed to God's cause and participate in His story.

One last observation about the relationship between Israel and Gibeon needs to be made. The Gibeonites deceived Joshua and the Israelite leaders resulting in a peace treaty built on false premises. In addition, at the time the treaty was made, God was not consulted about it, and the Israelites were duped by the Gibeonites. However, Joshua and the leaders' failure ultimately led to the protection and salvation of Gibeon from the Amorite kings. The treaty with Israel brought on the wrath of the kings, but the treaty also served to save the Gibeonites when they came under attack. When we speak of the promise of providence, we often underestimate its power. Even under false and cavalier pretenses, God was able to bring forth good both for Israel and for Gibeon. Our world is messy, and our decisions are often flawed. If we are faithful and continue to seek God, He works for our good not only in spite of our sin, but also through our sin. That is no small promise when, with the best of intentions, we make a huge mess of things either in our own life or in the life of others. Given time, God turns our messes into victories for His children.

Entering the Promised Land

Daily Reflection and Meditation

The Wonder and Healing of Providence

Recall and record a time when you made a mistake that God then turned into a blessing.

_____
_____
_____
_____
_____

Would you be more willing to take risks in serving Jesus Christ if you were fully convinced that even your mistakes and missteps would be used for good, both for you and for others? Why or why not? How would complete confidence in God's providence change you?

_____
_____
_____
_____
_____

When have you tried to repair a situation in your life without God's help, hoping He would not notice or would at least overlook your failure if you took care of it yourself?

_____
_____
_____

How did that work out for you?

The Painful Lessons of Victory

The book of Joshua continues with the complete conquest of the land, followed by the division of the land among the eleven tribes. The Levites did not receive land because they were priests. They were assigned cities throughout the land, which made it possible for them to teach and serve the people of Israel. It should be noted that, although the book of Joshua records a near-complete conquest of the Promised Land, a significant population of non-Israelites remained in the area. What Joshua conquered were major cities, particularly royal cities where kings were enthroned, and in this way established the supremacy of Israel. However, the destruction of the main cities did not include the various tribes, clans, and nomads that lived in pasturelands or hills throughout the territory. Many of these avoided being caught up in the wars for the cities simply by virtue of their "rural" locale. While Israel could claim victory over the entire land, that would not matter particularly to those on the periphery without substantial investment in the cities. As is seen in the book of Judges, conquering the land and settling the land were two different matters, and Israel was much more successful in the former than the latter.

These truths apply to us as well, and we need to know and expect "uprisings" in our lives, both from within and without. When we give ourselves over to Christ, our inclination is to believe that from that time on our lives will be less complicated because we are obedient and faithful. If only that were true… But the fact of the matter is that our journey of discipleship *is* the time when the Spirit begins to bring to the surface the conflicts and infidelities deep within us. Unhealthy (sinful) traits and attitudes we never considered or even realized were part of our thinking and loving become acutely obvious when we are invested in God's plans and intentionally pursue His wishes and goals in and for our lives. This is why we see people renowned for their faith and/or witness commit some outrageous sin that is eventually brought to light. While the revelation of our own weaknesses and failures may be less spectacular, if only because we are less public, we can be sure that these skirmishes will surface. Problems in the way we relate and, hence, in our relationships present themselves. Sexual sin comes to light. Judgmentalism, critical natures, jealousies, and a host of other less obvious sins that we call "just human nature" become obstacles both in our relationship to God and in our efforts to do His work. As painful as these are to see in ourselves, we do not need to be afraid of them. What we must realize is that God is claiming our heart and mind for Himself one step at a time. Likewise, we are being released from the bondage of the sinful nature one sin at a time. Early on in the studies we discussed the difference between holiness and virtue. Holiness is being set apart for God's purposes today and His overarching purpose of the salvation and redemption of His creation. Virtue, however, must be cultivated and grown, and that is what God is doing when He engages us in a battle for the hidden regions of our soul. We can give Christ our all, but when we do, He begins to reveal our "all" to us, much of which is not nearly as nice as we imagined it to be. We live with these faults and frailties of human nature without realizing that they keep us from being fully alive and free.

In the division of the land among the tribes of Israel, several smaller but no less important lessons remain. The tribe of Dan was the seventh lot assigned, but they were unable to claim all of their territory (19:40-48). When they were unsuccessful in claiming all the territory, they gave up and conquered another, easier city, leaving the people of other gods occupying a portion of their inheritance. No matter how much we grow, sin stays with us. We do not win every battle against sin, not even with God's help, because some sins are so deeply embedded within us that we do not let them be purged. That is not good, but it is true. Paul spoke of doing what he hated and not doing what he wanted to do,[5] and that applies to us as well. No matter how badly we wish we could 'be perfect as our Father in heaven is perfect,'[6] it won't happen, and we will disappoint ourselves and our Father. We are saved by grace, not by works, and inevitably, our works fall short and fail because the fullness of sin is never completely purged from our lives. When we "do what we hate,'" we need to repent, get up, dust ourselves off, and keep going. God is not surprised by our sin. Only we are surprised by it.

In Joshua's farewell speech to Israel, he reminded them of all that God had done for them beginning with the signs and wonders done in Egypt. He then called them again into covenant, reassuring them about the promise of God to be with them and to provide for and protect them. Joshua also warned them what would happen if they allied themselves and intermarried with the people

---

[5] cf. Romans 7:15.
[6] cf. Matthew 5:48.

remaining in the land. Chapter 23 records, "... you may be sure that the LORD your God will no longer drive out these nations before you. Instead, they will become snares and traps for you, whips on your backs and thorns in your eyes, until you perish from this good land, which the LORD your God has given you."

If we give in to our sin, eventually it will own us. We must choose a faithful and obedient relationship with Jesus Christ over and over again in our lives. It is so easy to become complacent, and when we do so, we end up in a quagmire of our own making, subjected by the sins we ignored and the relationship we compromised. The rich, blessed, sustaining relationship of abundance is lost to us. Made in the Image of God, we have free will and free choice. We can and do make decisions that serve us rather than Jesus Christ. If we are wise, we will accept the lesson we learn from our failures of disobedience or abandonment, and, as He did with Gibeon, God will use these for good. If we do not humble ourselves and admit our unfaithfulness, our sin will continue to ensnare us and trap us. We will instinctively choose situations and circumstances that are comfortable for our sin, and there we will find misery.

We are God's children, and He fights for us. He pursues us in our disobedience, both before and after we are born into His family. We can be sure that we will falter and fail, but who we are in Jesus Christ does not change. Our choices determine the extent to which we allow the Spirit to grow us. Many years ago, very early on in ministry, I was standing washing dishes at the kitchen sink singing along with hymns from a tape I enjoyed. As I sang with my all-time favorite hymn, *Holy, Holy, Holy,* the words of the second verse suddenly "appeared" before me. *"All the saints adore Thee, casting down their golden crowns around the glassy sea..."* Before me I saw a wizened old man whom I knew to be John Cassian, a lesser-known Early Church Father I had been reading. He was standing at the "shore of an indescribably beautiful glassy sea" bending down and lowering his crown, all the while looking at me and inviting me to give myself wholly to the Kingdom of God and my Father who lives and reigns there. A deep surge of longing welled up in me, but a part of me immediately recoiled as well. I had too much to lose in this world, or so I thought at the time. Whatever next step was in store for me, I will never know. What I do know is that God invested years of patient - and sometimes not-so-patient - ministry to me before I fully submitted to Him, if indeed I have yet. Do I wish I had made the right choice when it was offered so long ago? Yes, but that is based on what I now know to be true. I was too strong-willed, distrustful, and independent at the time to relinquish my whole heart and mind to Jesus Christ, even with the gift of a divine vision and invitation.

God does not dwell in "what ifs." However, neither does God abandon or forget us when we are rebellious and faithless. His love is everlasting, incomprehensible, and relentless. This is why we go through the struggles of growth in the life of Christ: so that we may live in the fullness of our Father's love, the only place we are finally safe, alive, joyful, and free. We do not pursue the Promised Land of God's Kingdom for God's benefit, although we do serve Him throughout our lives along the way. We pursue and struggle for the Kingdom of God because Life is there, and every deep longing of our hearts is satisfied only in the loving heart of God.

Entering the Promised Land

Daily Reflection and Meditation

The Painful Lessons of Victory

God abides in the Truth, and when we choose to follow Jesus Christ, the truth about our heart and mind is going to be revealed. What about that scares you? (If you do not experience at least some fear, then it is likely you are either not aware of or have not fully admitted to the depth of sin and/or idolatry in yourself.)

_____
_____
_____
_____
_____

Describe a time when your own sin harmed you and others.

_____
_____
_____
_____
_____

What sins has God purged from you in the past?

_____
_____
_____
_____

What sin is God working to break within you right now?

IV

The Physical Vices

Getting Serious About Sin

Thus far, discussion about sin has been limited almost exclusively to the sinful nature, primarily because the fallen nature of human beings is the disease that plagues everyone. Human nature as described in the Fall in Genesis 3 is a broad description of the fundamental problem with every person ever born. Throughout our lives, we will struggle between the will to sin and the will to obey, the desire for satisfaction of the self and the desire to be free in Jesus Christ. In the sense of the sinful nature, one sin is not differentiated from another. All are destructive. From the most egregious of sins – murder, for example – to more commonplace sins like selfishness, the sinful nature itself is the obstacle to the fullness of humanity as was seen in Jesus Christ. Paul wrote, "This righteousness from God comes through faith in Jesus Christ to all who believe. There is no difference, for all have sinned and fall short of the glory of God, and are justified freely by His grace through the redemption that came by Christ Jesus."[1] Paul's point is simply that we are saved by God's grace, redeemed by Jesus Christ, and we receive that salvation through faith. How good we are by comparison to one another is irrelevant because salvation is made possible only through Jesus Christ, not by our goodness or our good works. We know that.

However, early on in the life of the Early Church, some sins were recognized as more dangerous than others, at least within the context of the struggle to be purged of the sinful nature. These sins are variously known as mortal sins, cardinal sins, or deadly sins because, left unaddressed, they effectively block the work of the Holy Spirit in us, thus separating us from God and leading us toward hell. The Early Church Fathers understood the indulgence of these particular sins was deadly for life in Christ, and prevented individuals from enjoying full fellowship with God and becoming the reflection of Christ's glory. In its own way each of these sins reveal attachments to the world that must be broken if we are to participate fully in

---

[1] Romans 11:22-24.

the life of God. Is one sin worse than another? In terms of our salvation, the answer must be *no* because we all suffer from the sinful nature, at least when we are not enjoying the sinful nature.[2] Yet, some sins breed growing barriers between God and us, and these are the sins identified by the Early Church Fathers as the more treacherous sins of human nature. They are not, as we are inclined to think, specific actions as are found in the Ten Commandments: idolatry, murder, adultery, and the like. Rather, the mortal sins of human nature are common qualities and characteristics found in every person in some degree. Each is fertile soil for growing related sins and distancing us farther from God. Left unchecked, this separation from God will increase in spite of our prayers and often affect our prayer life itself. Deadly sins are a quagmire from which it is difficult to be extricated. If we cannot recognize these sins for what they are, they will continually stand as obstacles in our relationship with our Father, potentially destroying the relationship.

Jesus used the parable of the farmer sowing seeds[3] to describe the ways in which life in Him begins but is destroyed. Although He does not list specific sins, per se, the deadly sins fit within the various circumstances of the seed that prevented them from flourishing into plants. Jesus was not giving a lesson on farming. He used a parable to explain why some people mature in Christian faith and life while others do not. In effect He was naming mortal sins: lack of understanding, shallow roots of faith, and worldly cares. All of these undermine faith and certainly prevent maturation in discipleship. The Early Church Fathers simply identified those particular sins that have the effect Jesus described in the parable. If we want to grow in Christ and experience the freedom and joy of life in the Spirit, we must get serious about rooting out the deadly sins in our own lives.

---

[2] I make this distinction intentionally. The fact of the matter is, many of our sins seem quite pleasant to us, and we are attached to them, often as an expression of who we are. It is exactly this enjoyment of sin that makes these sins deadly. In its unique hold each deadly sin is appealing to us, which is what makes these sins so dangerous. We embrace them without thinking because we do not tend to see them as sins that keep us from enjoying God and hearing His call to abundant life in Him.

[3] Matthew 13:3-23.

Daily Reflection and Meditation

Getting Serious about Sin

We all agree that we are sinners, but we are less clear about specific sin in our lives. What root of sin is God working to pull out of your life right now?

_____

_____

_____

_____

_____

Jesus approached the lame man at the pool of Bethesda and asked him, "Do you want to get well?" If he were made well, the man essentially would have to become a different person, no longer lying in a state of disease. Do you want to get well? Do you want to become a person no longer in a state of dis-ease? Are you ready to become the person Christ can make you through the work of His Holy Spirit? Why or why not?

_____

_____

_____

_____

_____

John Cassian the Roman

The deadly sins have been discussed and written about throughout the history of the Church, and many writers and resources are available for exploring them. Typically, the seven sins are defined as mortal sins: pride, envy, gluttony, lust, anger, greed, and sloth. Teaching on the cardinal sins varies somewhat, but not in their significance and danger. Likewise, the order in which the sins are listed – and therefore, addressed – differs among writers. The sins themselves are consistent among writers, with one notable exception: John of Cassian. St. John Cassian, also known as Cassian the Roman, was a monk who lived circa AD 360 to 435 and is today a lesser-known Early Church Father. To say he was a monk does not do justice to the expanse of his life and experience. St. John Cassian traveled extensively and studied under some of the great men of his time, notably, Evagrios in Egypt and St. John Chrysostom in Constantinople. For a time he lived in Rome before moving to Gaul, where he founded a monastery for men and a monastery for women near Marseilles. The reason I chose St. John Cassian's writings as the basis for studying the sins is because he lists eight vices, not seven, adding self-esteem to his list of deadly sins. Self-esteem, ironically, is considered a great virtue in our society, which is why I believe it is important to study St. John Cassian's perspective on that quality.

A second reason for choosing the work of St. John Cassian is simply because of his approach. Most discussions on the cardinal sins begin with pride, understandably so, because pride is considered the root of our fall from grace. If one struggles continually against pride, then ostensibly, the rest of our sins inevitably will be addressed. In contrast, St. John Cassian began with the physical vices, sins of the flesh – or sins against the flesh – arguing that unless and until we can conquer the sins of the flesh, we lack the wherewithal to battle against spiritual sin, the sins of the heart and soul. He is not alone in that thought, and my inclination is to agree with him. Having said that, however, I do believe that we battle sin on many fronts, often concurrently, and seldom are we in a position to address one sin at a time. Still, moving through the sins in a systematic way gives order to our seeking and striving with the Holy Spirit.

If we desire to grow in the Holy Spirit and for the fruit of the Spirit to grow in us, then we need to realize that there are certain sins we need to strive to overcome. When we realize and acknowledge these sins, then we can work with the Holy Spirit to break the power they hold on us. The fruit of the Spirit comes from the Spirit. While discipline and determination may enable us to control these sins, they do not defeat them. Only the Spirit of God has the power to break the stranglehold of these sins – truly, any sin – in our lives. If we submit to the work of the Holy Spirit in us, if we work with Him in the battle against these sins, the Spirit of God in turn grows fruit where sin once was deeply rooted.

Not all sins apply equally to all people. Some sins have a stronger hold on some people while other sins are disproportionately present in different people. Such is the nature of humanity. We have different inclinations. Moreover, we may decide to address each sin in the order listed – indeed, we ought to attempt to do so – but it is the Holy Spirit Who correctly determines what sin to address when according to His perfect wisdom and mercy. Just as our good works are done in the power and under the direction of the Holy Spirit, so also should our internal work for release from the hold of sin be done with the Holy Spirit. God alone knows the steps we need to take, and we need to follow His lead and receive His help if we ever hope to conquer sin in our lives.

Daily Reflection and Meditation
John Cassian the Roman

Do you think some sins are more dangerous than others? Why or why not?

_____
_____
_____
_____
_____

Just looking at the cardinal sins, which do you think is most prominent in your life, and why?

_____
_____
_____
_____
_____

Now, pray for the Spirit to show you what He considers the most dangerous sin in your life at this time. Write down whatever comes to mind.

_____
_____
_____
_____
_____

Gluttony

Upon returning from a trip to a large city in a nation on another continent, a friend remarked that, "All the Americans were easy to pick out. They were the only fat people there." Regularly we hear about the "obesity epidemic" in the United States. There is good cause for that. An estimated thirty-five percent[4] of the American population is obese. We are in good company. Obesity is defined as having a Body Mass Index[5] over thirty. The thirty-five percent obesity rate does not include those who are simply overweight: individuals with a BMI of twenty-five to twenty-nine percent. These statistics perfectly illustrate the difference between suffering from sin and enjoying sin.

When the greatest spiritual gift a Christian can receive is love for others and when Jesus' own command was simply to love one another, we might wonder what difference obesity makes in our ability to love. The answer to this question applies to all the cardinal sins in some manner and is important for us to understand. Gluttony reveals two important obstacles to maturation as a Christian and thus, our ability to love: an unhealthy attachment to worldly things, and a consistent and continual effort to be filled and satisfied by the world. If we are to seek the greater life of Christ, we cannot be trying to fill ourselves first with worldly pleasures, in this case, specifically food. The reverse is true as well. If we seek satisfaction and contentment from food, then within us lies an emptiness that we will try to fill with other physical things, be it drink, comforts, wealth, or any number of material things. The point is less that we are obsessed with food than we have a spiritual yearning and barrenness that we are placating with food. Gluttony is the obvious symptom of a deeper hunger.

St. John Cassian lived as a monk in an earlier age. One of the results of overeating is obvious and was highly problematic in an agrarian community: listlessness and inattentiveness. After eating too much, monks preferred to take a nap instead of returning to the structured work and prayers that filled their days. We only have to consider what most people do after eating Thanksgiving dinner. Everyone lies around and watches television or naps until sufficient

---

[4] Center for Disease Control, http://www.cdc.gov/obesity/data/adult.html.
[5] Body Mass Index (BMI) is calculated by dividing weight by height squared and multiplying that number by 703. [WxH^2] x 703 = BMI.

energy for a walk returns. Beyond the practical problem of gluttony in a monastic community, which actually applies to our lives as well, there are spiritual dangers associated with gluttony. Paul warned that we are not to worry about how to satisfy the desires of the flesh, for in so doing, we are not focused on Christ.[6] Additionally, as alluded to above, we are seeking to be filled to abundance with food when the abundance that truly and completely satisfies comes from God, not from food or any other source. In his letter to the Philippians, Paul wrote, "For, as I have often told you before and now say again even with tears, many live as enemies of the cross of Christ. Their destiny is destruction, their god is their stomach, and their glory is in their shame. Their mind is on earthly things. But our citizenship is in heaven. And we eagerly await a Savior from there, the Lord Jesus Christ, Who, by the power that enables Him to bring everything under His control, will transform our lowly bodies so that they will be like His glorious body."[7]

It is no accident that obesity is found in epidemic proportion in the U.S. The more material and physical we are as a society, and hence, the less spiritually alive we are, the greater is our need for satisfaction. The increase in obesity in the last fifty years or so goes hand-in-hand with the increase in drug and alcohol abuse and inversely correlates to the decline in interest in and understanding of spiritual matters and the spiritual life. Professionals debate nature vs. nurture in the rise of obesity, and medical research looks for naturalistic causes and solutions: genetics, pharmaceutical solutions, and surgeries. Physical solutions address the physical problem, but gluttony is a condition of the heart and soul – the desire, even need, to fill a hole, cover a wound, or hide a fear within us. Babies do not overeat. Dissatisfied, bored, and/or hurting children and adults overeat. But dissatisfaction, boredom, and pain are not from God. He provides the healing, meaning, purpose, and sufficiency that make us whole. Regardless of one's genetics or the eating habits of one's childhood, gluttony is finally a spiritual problem, not a physical problem. Obesity is only the symptom.

The solution, then, should be obvious in part. Seeking Christ in prayer is the first step in overcoming gluttony. In fact, seeking the fullness of life in God

---

[6] cf. Romans 13:14. *Flesh* is also translated *sinful nature*, depending upon the translation.
[7] Philippians 3:18-21.

is the first step in combating any and all sin, including the remaining deadly sins. The second step we need to take is intentional fasting. Fasting is not done for the purposes of losing weight. We undertake fasting to break our attachment to the world and to attach our heart, mind, and soul to Jesus Christ. Interestingly, St. John Cassian warned against fasting for long periods of time because hunger can produce the same listlessness and lack of energy as gluttony. Rather, the goal of fasting is the right ordering of our appetites. Fullness comes from God. Food sustains the body. When our spiritual appetite is rightly ordered, that is, directed toward God, then our appetite for food will decline proportionately. God gave us food to sustain us. I do not believe He intends for us not to enjoy food, but food cannot be the source of fulfillment for us. Jesus Himself said, "Life is more than food, and the body more than clothes."[8] More significantly, Jesus also said, "I am the Bread of Life. He who comes to Me will never go hungry, and he who believes in Me will never be thirsty."[9] When we are satisfied by the life that comes from the Spirit of Christ, gluttony will no longer have a hold over us. It will not be necessary. By fasting, we submit to work with the Holy Spirit to draw life from Christ, not from food.

Truly Christ-like love flows from the love of God that fills us. If we are seeking to fill ourselves with the world, specifically food, it is nigh on impossible to be filled with love. Gluttony damages maturation as a Christian, and therefore, also diminishes our capacity to love others.[10]

---

[8] Luke 12:.23.
[9] John 6:35.
[10] This statement implies that, in some sense, overweight people are unable to love fully as mature Christians, a statement surely offensive to the overweight. Be that as it may, gluttony does inhibit our relationship with God, in much the same manner that any sin does the same. Gluttony is a mortal sin precisely *because* it prevents maturation as a Christian, since we are seeking to satisfy our spiritual thirst and hunger with food.

Daily Reflection and Meditation

Gluttony

Is there evidence of gluttony in your life? If yes, how so?

_____
_____
_____
_____
_____

What are other ways, besides food, in which you try to satisfy yourself – alcohol, for example? Ask God to show you ways in which you try to fill your soul with something other than Him.

_____
_____
_____
_____
_____

What is the difference between fasting and dieting?

_____
_____
_____
_____
_____

The Physical Vices

If you struggle with gluttony, are you willing to start practicing fasting on a regular basis? If so, what are your expectations?

_____
_____
_____
_____
_____
_____

Lust

Lust in our culture knows virtually no bounds. There is not even the pretense of sexual control in contemporary social attitudes. At least with gluttony, there is some sense of the undesirability of obesity, if for no other reason than the health risks associated with it. But lust? Lust is practically trumpeted as the zenith of our humanity and individual self-expression. Ostensibly, lust leads to love, but that is seldom the case. Lust is simply lust: self-indulgent sexual desire. The very definition belies the essence of the self-giving love necessary for lifetime commitment and nurture. The fruit of lust abounds in sexually transmitted diseases, unwanted pregnancies, abortions, extramarital affairs, divorces, pornography, troubled children and youths, and more. In spite of the obvious complications of unrestrained lust, our society blindly ignores the inherent dangers of sexual "freedom" even as we become increasingly enslaved to our sexual appetites. Unreserved sexual innuendo and/or activity are present almost every time the television is on. A few years ago a rice company marketed a new line of pre-seasoned rice side dishes as obvious preludes to sexual satisfaction. Rice? Really? When did rice become an aphrodisiac? One can reasonably argue that we are an over-sexed society when the promise of sexual fulfillment sells rice.

A full discussion of the dubious nature of our attitudes toward human sexuality is beyond the scope of our immediate topic, but suffice it to say that the current opinions about sexual self-expression began when we decided lust was a good thing. Yet, there is a reason that the Church has historically believed and taught that lust is a deadly sin.[11] Lust is the opposite of all things Christ-like because it is self-indulgent, and lust is specifically self-indulgent in the objectification of someone else. In other words, lust seeks to satisfy the self through the use of another. This is in total contradiction to the call to lay down our lives for one another.[12] We cannot use a person for the gratification of our

---

[11] I qualify the Church's belief and teaching with "historically" because the contemporary church barely pays lip service to traditional Christian teaching regarding sexual behavior. The widespread acceptance of and participation in sexual activity outside the marriage covenant have created a large gap between what we say we believe and what we actually teach and practice. Sermons on sexuality are rare at best, and beyond the occasional class on sexuality provided for adolescents, sexual conduct is virtually never discussed.

[12] cf. 1 John 3:16.

sexual desire one moment and the next, successfully sacrifice ourselves for the good of that same person. Humbling and emptying ourselves after the example of Christ are incompatible with lust. We cannot be both self-denying and self-gratifying, most especially when we gratify ourselves at the expense of another, even a willing partner in lust. Encouraging another's lust to satisfy our own is not in any sense encouraging their full humanity in Jesus Christ.

Sexual desire is strong in human beings, and God did not accidentally create us with that desire. Moreover, the very fact that sexual intercourse is not only desirable, but also highly enjoyable reveals that God fully intended for us to be sexual beings. Having said that, animals are sexual beings as well. What distinguishes human beings from animals is the place and meaning in which God ordained the sexual satisfaction of human beings. Animals lust during mating season. Sex between human beings as God ordered in our creation is the joining of two persons into one. Thus, when we randomly satisfy our sexual appetite – when we satiate our lust – two do not become one, but rather, we become one with a half-dozen different people, with twenty different people, or with however many individuals with whom we have sexual intercourse throughout our lives. The intimacy of the union God designed for our blessing – and our sexual satisfaction – is flagrantly discarded. Moreover, sex within marriage is the complete self-giving of each to the other, precisely the opposite of the self-gratification of lust.

Lust has an object, a person we see as the means to the end of sexual gratification. Whenever we objectify another human being, it is a form of lust, and it is also a denial of the Image of God in that person. Lust is not limited solely to sexual desire. Any time we see another human being as the means to an end for ourselves, for our personal satisfaction or gain, we are lusting. That is a broader definition than we typically consider, but the broader definition helps us understand why sexual lust is deadly. Every time we use another person to get something for ourselves, we are denying the inherit worth and value of that person. Each person we meet in every day of our lives is a person for whom Christ died and who is the beloved of our Father. To use others for our own satisfaction and fulfillment, for any reason, is an affront to the One Who loves them and made them in His Image for fellowship and communion with Him.

It is impossible to mature in Christian life and faith when we use the people we are called to love and serve as Christ loved and served. The longer we tolerate lust as an acceptable human trait, the greater is its hold on us. Lust is definitely a human trait, but it is a perversion born of the Fall. The Holy Spirit can break the hold of lust if we truly desire to be free. Not lusting does not mean we have no sexual desire. Rather, not lusting means that we have no desire to satisfy our sexual urges at the expense of others. This truly is the work of the Holy Spirit, and we have to make the decision that we want to be free of lust so we are free to love selflessly – without regard for sex or the intent to have sex to satisfy our desires. Like all sins, lust is hard to overcome, but through prayer and dependence upon and submission to the Holy Spirit, lust can be defeated. We must truly desire to love as Christ loves, and if that is our prayer, the Spirit will make possible what is impossible for us.[13] When lust arises in our heart and mind, we need to go to Christ Jesus in prayer right then, not to entertain the urges and thus feed them. Prayer for release from unhealthy desire opens us to the work of the Spirit within us to purify our desires and correctly aim our relationship to other persons.

---

[13] I hope I have successfully drawn the distinction between God-given sexual desire and lust. Desire for the opposite sex is not unhealthy or sinful. Lust is the use of another human being for the satisfaction of one's sexual desire. These are very different states of heart and mind. God intends for sexual desire to be satisfied in the confines of the self-giving bonds of marriage.

The Physical Vices

Daily Reflection and Meditation

Lust

Do you struggle with lust? If yes, then how is lust manifested in your life?

_____
_____
_____
_____
_____
_____

Why, if sexual desire is given to us by God in our creation, is lust an obstacle to full humanity?

_____
_____
_____
_____
_____
_____

Are there other ways besides lust in which you treat people as objects – usable for your satisfaction or benefit? Ask the Holy Spirit to show you times when you have used people without regard for their humanity.

_____
_____
_____
_____
_____
_____

If you struggle with lust, do you want to be released from it? Why or why not?

Greed

Of all the topics on which Jesus spoke, money was the second most frequent. Only the Kingdom of God was more frequently spoken of by Jesus. There is a reason for that: money buys security in every century and civilization. The more money one has, the greater one's ability to provide for oneself from basic essentials like food and shelter to protection for one's family to extravagant luxuries. *Need* is relatively defined – relative to one's capacity to purchase. Why greed is considered a cardinal sin should be obvious to us. The more one has, the more likely one is to depend upon what one owns rather than on Christ. Because our world is never truly safe or predictable, money and possessions will never be sufficient for guaranteed security. Some years ago, I saw a study that I cannot now locate for documentation, but the thing that I remember about it was the universal desire for more income across the spectrum of income levels. Regardless of the amount of annual income, the people in every income bracket believed they would be content if they made just a little more money every year. Whether in the lowest bracket, about $20,000 per year, or the highest bracket, above $1,000,000 per year, every income segment indicated that more income was needed in order to be content.

The attitude of Christians toward money is drawn, probably unintentionally and even subconsciously, from the society in which we live. We are enthralled with money and material things, homes, cars, and possessions. Even if we do not have money, we purchase on credit. The Federal Reserve reported in April of 2019 that the amount of household debt exceeded $1.06 trillion, noticeably reduced since 2010, but not including $1.5 trillion in student debt. According to the American Bank Association, there are approximately 364,000,000 credit cards in circulation in the United States, and of the families that have credit card debt, the average amount of debt is over $6,500.[14] If we define greed as a persistent drive to acquire more than one needs, then, far from being a deadly sin, greed has become almost a virtue in our society, and is most certainly a way of life.

---

[14] All data is sourced through creditcard.com, and credit card debt necessarily fluctuates with the economy, unemployment, economic policies, and other factors. For the latest data, see: https://www.creditcards.com/credit-card-news/credit-card-statistics.php.

Attachment to material possessions and the accumulation of wealth permeate our culture and, I believe, correlate with the decline in personal faith among Americans. On any given Sunday morning, less than twenty-percent of the population attends church. If we as a society have little or no confidence in the providence and provision of God, then of necessity, we must have confidence in self-provision. Thus, absent faith in a loving and sufficient God, the accumulation of wealth is virtually a necessity. However, there is not much evidence that the spending habits of church-goers are any different from the spending habits of non-church-goers.

Greed and materialism are an unhealthy attachment to the physical realm to the ignorance or exclusion of spiritual matters. Paul wrote to Timothy, "For the love of money is a root of all kinds of evil. Some people, eager for money, have wandered from the faith and pierced themselves with many griefs."[15] The greatest evil is separation from God, and if we attach ourselves to that which is physical, we necessarily are not attached to that which is spiritual. Yes, Paul's point was not that money is bad, only the love of money, but the measure of our relief in that distinction is itself the revelation of the depth of our personal attachment to money. Money is not bad. Good things can be and are done with money. We all need a place to live and food to eat, but what is sufficient? How much is enough? Our answer will tell us something about the presence of greed in our lives. Jesus was quite clear about human greed. "No servant can serve two masters. Either he will hate the one and love the other, or he will be devoted to the one and despise the other. You cannot serve both God and Money."[16] God and money *are* the contrast between that which is eternal and everlasting and that which is finite and temporary. We cannot serve both. One will master us, and we must decide which it will be.

A good friend decided his life was too full of "stuff." Stuff is distracting and demanding, and after thought, prayer, and discussion with his wife, my friend and his family moved into a smaller home. He began shopping for clothing at second-hand stores and traded his late-model vehicle for a lesser means of transportation. Why? Because most of the time, the stuff we own owns us more than we realize. What he needs is actually significantly less than

---

[15] 1 Timothy 6:10.
[16] Luke 16:13.

what he has. That is true for all of us, but we rebel at the idea of ridding ourselves of excess because our belongings offer us security, comfort, and even identity.

His response to the realization of the prominence of material things in his life is the correct answer to greed: giving away what we do not need. There is nothing wrong with having a decent home in a safe neighborhood, but what constitutes sufficient? The Lord told Paul, "My grace is sufficient for you, for My power is made perfect in weakness." Therefore I will boast all the more gladly about my weaknesses, so that Christ's power may rest on me."[17] How will we ever learn that Christ is sufficient for all that we need if we provide ourselves with all that we want? How will we even come to know what we truly need, as opposed to the many things we want?

Money funds the church and every good work that we do. Money is not the problem. Our attachment to money is the problem, and in our society love of money and all that it buys is constantly encouraged. Yet, this attitude and these very things keep us from drawing closer to God, depending upon Him, and investing ourselves in what is eternal and eternally important. Greed is an obstacle to life, not an answer to life. The way to overcome greed is intentional generosity. Whether it be cash or belongings, we need to give away all that is more than we require. Jesus said, "But store up for yourselves treasures in heaven, where moth and rust do not destroy, and where thieves do not break in and steal. For where your treasure is, there your heart will be also."[18] If we treasure possessions, we cannot treasure Christ and the life He gives.

---

[17] 2 Corinthians 12:9.
[18] Matthew 6:20-21.

Daily Reflection and Meditation
Greed

Make a list of your belongings that you treasure. Look around your home and in your life. What is important to you? From retirement funds to photographs, try to create as complete a list as possible of the things that matter to you.

_____
_____
_____
_____
_____
_____

How many of the things listed above do you need to survive?

_____
_____
_____
_____
_____
_____

If God asked you to give away everything you do not need, would you? Why or why not?

_____
_____
_____
_____
_____
_____

The Physical Vices

God wants all idols in our lives to be destroyed. If we treasure anything more than our eternal relationship with Him, He wants us to get rid of it. Can you? Why or why not?

_____

_____

_____

_____

Jesus said, "And why do you worry about clothes? See how the lilies of the field grow. They do not labor or spin. Yet I tell you that not even Solomon in his entire splendor was dressed like one of these. If that is how God clothes the grass of the field, which is here today and tomorrow is thrown into the fire, will He not much more clothe you, O you of little faith? (Matthew 6.28-30) Do you believe Jesus really meant what He said? Will God provide sufficiently for even your most basic needs?

_____

_____

_____

_____

If you responded "no," what does that reveal about your relationship with Jesus Christ, and why do you think so?

_____

_____

___

___

___

If you responded 'yes,' are you preparing to divest yourself of excess? Why or why not?

___

___

___

___

___

___

V

The Five Vices of the Soul

Unless and until we have overcome, or at least have become aware of and are struggling against the physical vices, we cannot begin to struggle against the spiritual vices. St. John Cassian understood vices as demons[1] that provoke our weaknesses, causing them to grow and destroy life in Jesus Christ. God the Spirit is the "Doctor of our souls." The struggle against these vices is entirely internal, not external, and these vices are the cause of our sinful and evil choices.

Anger

"My dear brothers, take note of this: Everyone should be quick to listen, slow to speak and slow to become angry, for man's anger does not bring about the righteous life that God desires."[2] Most of us have experienced the destructive force of anger, whether on the giving end or the receiving end. A story is told of the father who, wishing to teach his son to control his temper, required him to hammer a nail into a fence post every time he lost his temper at someone or over something. Over time, the number of nails on the fence post grew until it was nearly covered. But as the boy grew as well, he worked to overcome his temper, and every time he apologized and made amends for losing his temper, his father allowed him to remove a nail from the post. One

---

[1] St. Nikodemos of the Holy Mountain and St. Makarios of Corinth. *The Philokalia, Volume 1,* Trans (from Greek) by G.E.H. Palmer in Philip Sherrard, Kallistos Ware. (1983) (London: Faber Paperbacks, 1983) 73-93. With the use of the word "demons," Cassian did not intend to remove personal responsibility from the battle for the soul. Demons – the demonic, evil, however one prefers to think of it – appeal to our weaknesses. They quite literally lead us into temptation and then encourage pre-existent sin in us. However, no demon can force us to act short of demonic possession (if in fact such a thing as full possession is possible). As we do with God Almighty, we maintain our free will with the evil one and demonic influences. The choice to refuse or succumb to sin is always ours. "The devil made me do it" is not a legitimate excuse to offer our Father when we sin.

[2] James 1:19-20.

day as the two were outside together, they happened by the fencepost. The father stopped and looked at it, deep in thought. Calling his son closer to the fence post, the father leaned down and pointed out how many of the nails had been removed and congratulated his son for making apologies and doing the right thing. But then he went on to point out that the holes made by each removed nail were still in the fence post. Once we get angry and wound others with our temper, there is no taking it back. We can apologize and make amends, but the damage is already done.

We think little of anger. It is a common human emotion. Most of us are acutely aware of the hurts we receive as a result of someone else's anger, yet we tend to accept our own anger as an inevitability, often quite justified, and a simple fact of life. However, anger does great harm, not only to those toward whom our anger is aimed regardless of how justified we might be in our anger, but also within us. Anger is a destructive emotion, both to those on whom it is visited and on those who are angry. Paul went so far as to write, "In your anger do not sin: Do not let the sun go down while you are still angry, and do not give the devil a foothold."[3] How many times in life have we lain in bed at night and tossed and turned in anger at another, rehearsing all the things we would like to say as soon as we have the opportunity? But Paul understood that feeding our anger is an invitation for the destruction of others and ourselves that the devil so enjoys breeding.

Today, we are encouraged to express our anger, to get it out, and not allow it to fester within us. No doubt, this is good advice because festering anger is just as damaging to us as an eruption of anger aimed at another. Yet, that is not what Paul and James were counseling, nor is the expression of anger what God desires for us. God wants to eradicate anger, not get it out in the open so it is unleashed on someone else. No matter how justified our anger may be, it is always destructive.

St. John Cassian taught that we are to seek to reject all anger through prayer and to apologize without regard to whether we are right or wrong. The goal is to restore the relationship with the one toward whom we are angry. If we walk away out of anger, we have to go back. Anger that is removed by isolation is not anger that is removed from the soul. If we isolate ourselves in order to

---

[3] Ephesians 4:26-27.

avoid being angry – for example, avoiding someone who angers us – then all we have succeeded in doing is removing the provocation, not the root of anger within us. What is more important for the healing of our soul is ridding ourselves of angry thoughts and ill-will toward our neighbor, toward the one who angers us, rather than simply learning to control the outburst of anger. God sees the state of our soul, our intentions and motivations, not our actions. Just as good works flow from who we are in Jesus Christ, so do sinful works flow from who we are not in Jesus Christ. Anger derives from sin within us, as well as from the absence of humility.

Anger is a secondary emotion. It never springs up as an independent emotion but arises from an unnamed primary emotion that we experience. That primary emotion can be insecurity, arrogance, pride, self-hate, too much self-love, and the list goes on. There are a host of underlying emotions that cause us to respond in anger, but at its root, anger can be traced back to two fundamental facts about the state of our soul: we lack humility about ourselves, or we lack trust in the love of God, or some combination thereof. The first state responds angrily when our pride is insulted or our high opinion of ourselves is brought into question. Distrust in God's good and providential love for us is expressed in anger when we are insecure, afraid, or full of self-hate. It is this primary emotion or emotions that the Spirit desires to heal in us, and allowing anger to fester is an obstacle to the truth about ourselves and the truth about the state of our souls.

Paul also wrote to the Ephesians, "Get rid of all bitterness, rage and anger, brawling and slander, along with every form of malice."[4] All of these are expressions of the sinful nature, harming others through us and preventing our maturation as Christians. Anger especially blinds the eye of the soul. Just as we have creative vision or are able to discern the signs of the time politically, so also do we have spiritual vision, and anger obstructs spiritual vision. When we are angry, we cannot discern the mind of Christ, nor can we understand the things of God.

It is interesting to note that of all the things Jesus trained the disciples to do – teach, preach, heal, cast out evil, even bring people back to life – the one

---

[4] Ephesians 4:31.

thing Jesus did alone was cleanse the Temple.[5] The cleansing of the moneychangers from the Temple is often cited as an example of Jesus' righteous anger. Yet, the texts do not say that He was angry. Moreover, even if He was, He did not invite His disciples to participate. If He was indeed angry, it was with the perfect righteousness that belongs to God alone, and God's anger is not like our anger, for God's righteousness is beyond compare to our own. One other obvious point to make is that God alone gets to decide who is invited to stay and who is not welcome in His house.

The first thing we need to do in combating anger is decide we do not want to be angry or to get angry. We have to agree with the Scriptures and commit ourselves to eradicating anger from our heart and soul. Once we have made this commitment, every time anger arises within us – for whatever reason – we need to pray, right then, right there. Used through the centuries in various forms, the Jesus Prayer is a brief breath prayer that reminds us of our correct posture before God. "Lord Jesus Christ, Son of God, have mercy on me, a sinner, and save me." We are healed through prayer and repentance, and this particular prayer has proven beneficial for countless Christians over the centuries. Even as we confess our sinfulness and repent, we are seeking Christ's healing mercy.

I do not believe there is truly righteous anger, for we are never truly righteous people. The hardest anger for us to overcome is toward those who have hurt someone we love. But even as that anger is born out of our love and concern, we need to realize the anger arises out of a lack of faith in God's providential work in the lives of our loved one. We want justice or revenge by our own hand instead of trusting in God's love for our family member or friend. Even this anger is not righteous anger. All anger is wrong and is an obstacle to our relationship with and growth in Christ.

---

[5] cf. Matthew 21:12-13; Mark 11:15-17; Luke 19:45-46.

Daily Meditation and Reflection
Anger

What makes you angry?

_____
_____
_____
_____
_____

Ask the Holy Spirit to help you take an inventory of your soul. About what or with whom are you angry right now? Why?

_____
_____
_____
_____
_____

Anger is a source of power and control in our lives. What would you lose if you never got angry?

_____
_____
_____
_____
_____

Do you want to be free from anger? Explain your answer.

_____
_____
_____
_____
_____

Dejection

Dejection is the traditional word used for the malady of depression that is so prevalent in the United States today. Mental health professionals diagnose and treat depression with medication, and I do not want to challenge the science of pharmaceutical treatment of depression. There is no doubt that some people experience serious and/or chronic depression and that medication helps these people. However, anti-depressants are the most widely prescribed class of medicines in the United States, meaning that more people are taking medications for depression than there are people taking medication for heart disease, diabetes, cancer, or any other disease in the country. In what follows I will discuss depression as a spiritual malady, which I believe it is, but I do *not* endorse stopping medication for the treatment of depression. Spiritual growth and healing can lead to relief from depression, but until such healing has occurred – and I do believe Christ heals – it is dangerous to stop medications that assist in maintaining mental health in the interim. Using a two-pronged approach to mental health is no different from using a two-pronged approach with our physical health. We utilize doctors, medicines, and the latest technology for our bodies even as we pray for God's healing power in our lives and bodies. The same logic should also be applied to the healing of depression.

Let us start, specifically, by addressing the issue of the soul. As science has shaped the medical profession over the last centuries, the understanding of the human being morphed into a purely physical phenomenon. In other words, everything human might not yet be understood, but in due time, science and medical knowledge would prevail. This vein of thought underlies almost everything we presume to know about the human being in medicine and through science. Yet, the essence of our humanity is the soul. Because the soul is given by God and is the foremost place of union with Him in this life, we cannot understand what it means to be human independently of the reality of the soul. But this is precisely what medicine and science seek to do – to understand the human being as purely material – body, brain, emotions measured by brain waves, and the like. In light of naturalistic explanations of the origin of human beings, most pronounced in Darwin and developed through evolutionary theory, we should not be surprised by the decline of interest in all things spiritual, including the soul, nor by the dismissal of all things spiritual. The relationship between psychology/mental health and the spiritual life of human beings is an inverse correlation. In effect, the decline of interest in and discussion of the soul and the spiritual life corresponds almost exactly to an increase in interest in mental health, psychology, and psychiatry.

Not surprisingly, large segments of the population, sometimes estimated up to a quarter of the entire population, are being treated for depression with medication. I do not think it is coincidental that depression has increased as the prominence of faith in American life has decreased. To differentiate the despondency of serious depression from lesser types of depression that are also frequently treated by medication, we can speak of the latter as "situational" depression.[6] For our purposes here, we are referring primarily to situational depression. Circumstances, events, and relationships combine to create an oppressive affect in our heart, mind, and soul.

The challenge for us is that Christianity historically has held that dejection or depression is a sin, indeed, a mortal sin, for it kills the soul. Two comments: first, as just stated, we have ceased to look for the role of the soul and its impact on the human person and experience. Second, sin is more correctly understood as a disease in itself, the inevitable outcome of which is death. Thus, all sin is best understood as disease and best treated with spiritual practices and spiritual disciplines. Christians ought never to be pointing fingers at sin in others, but instead, to exhibit compassion for the deadly infection against which we all battle, including depression. The least helpful thing we can do is add to the burden of a depressed individual by suggesting the problem is simply one of sin that will be fixed through prayer and repentance. In every Christian's life, these practices are necessary, but healing is rarely immediate and frequently not complete.

Even so, the Church has long acknowledged the dangers of dejection, especially as that relates to our fellowship with Jesus Christ and our life and ministry in Him. One would be hard-pressed to argue that depression does not

---

[6] This term is not intended to diagnose, but to differentiate. All depression is not the same, and for our purposes in spiritual maturation, I want us to look at the varying ways in which we experience depression and the corresponding manner by which mental health professionals address depression vs. the manner by which Christians ought rightly to consider the difficulties of dejection.

kill the soul when an estimated fifteen-percent of those who suffer from major depressive disorder and/or clinical depression die by suicide. Serious depression is a beast of its own and afflicts a much smaller portion of the number of people diagnosed with depression. While I do not feel at all qualified to speak to the treatment of chronic depression as a medical condition, I do know that, as with all disease and illness, the presence of the Holy Trinity in our lives dramatically improves the quality of our lives. There is no reason to assume that the same is not true of major depressive disorder. An individual may require medication for chronic clinical depression for the entirety of his/her life, but as with any chronic disease, the presence of the light and life of Jesus Christ buoys the soul in spite of the body's well-being.[7]

Jesus said, "The eye is the lamp of the body; so then if your eye is clear, your whole body will be full of light. But if your eye is bad, your whole body will be full of darkness. If then the light that is in you is darkness, how great is the darkness!"[8] Jesus knew when He looked through His eyes, He was not seeing His stomach or lungs or any inward part of His body. Instead, the "eye" of the body is the attitude of the *nous*, the lens through which we see the world and interpret events. The Greek word used for *clear* is *aplous* and means not only physically sound eyesight, but also implies a state of the soul – of generosity and goodness. In the same way, the Greek root word translated as *bad* means not just physically impaired, but wicked or malicious. These are states of the soul, not merely emotions, reactions, or responses. When we refuse to acknowledge the soul, we leave the deepest, eternal essence of our humanity in the dark – quite literally. Treating emotions, habits, thoughts, interpretive patterns, and more without reference to the soul is akin to treating symptoms rather than the disease. I would strongly argue that the reason our society is living in an epidemic of depression is because we do not recognize

---

[7] Psychiatrists and mental health professionals classify major depressive disorder and/or clinical depression as an illness to be treated with medication, and evidence from brain scans supports the argument that those who suffer from clinical depression are suffering from a physical malfunction in the brain. I do not question that conclusion at all. My point is simply that we should *not* accept the foregone conclusion of professionals that this is a chronic disease without any relief. Medication may be necessary for the rest of a person's life, but we are looking at the healing power of the Gospel, which is 'foolishness to worldly authorities' but the power of salvation for Christians.

[8] Matthew 6:22-24.

the soul's existence, nor do we remember we are spiritual beings as well as physical or material beings. Without any intention of malfeasance, the human soul has atrophied through neglect, simply because we have forgotten we possess a soul.

Additionally, depression – especially situational, such as loss of a job, death of a family member, an accident or illness – turns our focus inward. This is completely reasonable, but this is also a potentially dangerous turn. While we must adapt to changes as they occur, particularly unwanted changes, constant focus on the self can start us on a downward spiral. The inward investment of time and energy can be helpful for adjusting, and for this reason, we see professional counselors and take medication to ease our woundedness during difficult times. However, avoiding all pain is unhealthy, as is maintaining an inward focus on the self. Let us think about the latter phrase first. Various adages and truisms from the past come to mind: depression is the catalyst for change; when feeling "blue" or sad, get up and go do something for someone else, and finally, the best way to beat depression is action. Each of these trivial sayings holds nuggets of surprising wisdom.

Constant self-reflection and self-absorption actually lead us deeper into depression because we are focused on what is wrong, what we have lost, or how we are hurt. The more we look at ourselves, the more deeply engaged with the self we become. Paul wrote, "For we are [God's] workmanship, created in Christ for good works, which God prepared beforehand so that we would walk in them."[9] "We are created for good works" means we will be most alive and vibrant when we are doing good for others. Secular society is consumed by the self, and this is a trap into which Christians cannot fall. Constantly testing our feelings and emotions is deeply unhealthy for the soul that thrives in doing good with and for others. Yes, our situation can be depressing when our plans and dreams are taken from us, especially if it happens abruptly. But the most effective antidote is not continual reflection on what we wish had happened or were different. Instead, getting up and making the effort to think of someone else, coming up with an idea for helping another, or finding a way of serving a person in need are all ways in which to turn life toward the good and to focus on the possibilities available in Jesus Christ.

---

[9] Ephesians 2:10.

That leads to the prior point that "avoiding all pain is unhealthy." Sometimes, we need to grieve a closed door. We need to cry for what we lost. Pain reminds us that we live and that life matters. What we do, the dreams we have, the people we love, all of these *matter*. To ignore the depth of loss or hurt or woundedness is to forfeit the potential for maturation, growth in Christ, and compassion for others. Sometimes, medication is the best way to assist us through dark times, and there is nothing wrong with that. What is wrong, however, is not to seek the healing power of the Spirit in our lives. Medication is a valuable aid when we are truly wounded, whatever the cause may be. As Christians, we misuse the medication if we do not take advantage of the relief it provides and turn to Christ Jesus to be healed. Anti-depressant medication can be an enormously beneficial aid while we cope with deep sadness in our hearts and minds. However, we want to cope temporarily, so *we can be healed*.

Finally, regarding clinical depression, both of the above apply to this more serious and lasting form of depression, but only to a degree. Every human being experiences meaning and joy in being with and doing for others. We were *created* to do so. But when the brain malfunctions – much like a pancreas in the body of a diabetic or the lungs in an asthmatic – then medication will likely always be necessary, and that is fine. Such depression should be fought in much the same manner as any disease, including lifestyle changes such as those discussed above when dealing with milder or more temporary causes of depression, but also with every applicable medical and pharmaceutical treatment available. We are wrong when we tell people who are depressed that they simply should pray more. We would not accuse an individual with cancer of being at fault and neither should we accuse an individual with major depressive disorder of being at fault. Instead, we should come alongside these individuals with compassion and care, encouragement and prayer.

Without any knowledge of contemporary mental health, St. John Cassian's understanding of dejection provides a remarkably clear and uniquely Christian perspective on depression, including overcoming depression in our lives. Dejection darkens the soul and prevents us from praying and turning to Christ for help and hope. It slowly eats away at the soul, making space for other vices to grow and/or increase, and we become bitter and lethargic. Depression also can be a source of sin. The most notable example of that is Judas. Following his betrayal of Christ,[10] Judas confessed that he had betrayed innocent blood. When the religious authorities were indifferent to his plea, Judas despaired and gave up hope. At that point he hanged himself. Judas' death was evil's final victory over him.

In the same way, when we do not resist depression, we allow ourselves to be drawn further and further away from Christ Jesus and the hope He gives us. It does not matter that we do this unintentionally. Knowing that the Holy Spirit can help us in the struggle against depression is the key to seeking the spiritual healing we need. Genuine hope and promise come from God, and we need to seek Him when life feels overwhelming. The truth of the matter is that, whatever our circumstances, they are not greater than God.

Speaking to the problem of depression, Paul wrote, "Godly sorrow brings repentance that leads to salvation and leaves no regret, but worldly sorrow brings death."[11] His point is that when we embrace worldly sorrow – when we are depressed about events and circumstances – it leads us first to the darkening of the soul and ultimately to spiritual death. The only appropriate sorrow of the soul is sorrow for sin, and the remedy for that sorrow is the forgiveness we receive from Christ. We can and should be deeply grieved by the sin in our lives, but once we have confessed our sin and repented, the grief and weight of sin should be lifted. If it is not, then we have not truly accepted the full forgiveness offered by Jesus Christ through the Cross.

When we struggle with depression, especially depression brought on by events in our lives, we are healed by prayer and by hope in God. Probably not surprisingly, when we are depressed, we are less likely to want to pray or to feel like kneeling before God in supplication. Dejection causes us to lose interest in that which gave us joy and purpose in other circumstances. Thus, when we most need the healing power of our God, we are the least likely to seek it. Meditation on the Scripture often reminds us of God's faithfulness, and the promise of new life and hope in Him. Likewise, being with godly people, people who live the joy of God's hope and promise, is a healing balm for depression. We feed our depression when we avoid being around others who have faith and hope when our own wanes. This is the point that is probably the

---

[10] Matthew 27:3-5.
[11] 2 Corinthians 7:10.

most important for us to take away from this topic: we are given spiritual tools to assist us, and we are to fight against depression rather than succumb to it. Because depression is common in our culture, we think nothing of it from a spiritual perspective. But that in itself is the lesson here: just because depression is commonly found does not make it inevitable or acceptable. With God's help, we can and should struggle against depression. When needed, we definitely should utilize the medical remedies available to us, but we should not rely on those alone, instead seeking the healing of hope that comes from Christ alone.

For depression to be lifted or removed, true healing can only come from the presence of Spirit in us and the hope that Christ gives us. Even then, not everyone will experience full or complete healing, but everyone can experience a measure of relief from the intense darkness associated with depression and/or dejection. This is what our Father wants for us. God does not desire that we live under the suffocating blanket of despair and gloom. He is perpetually and eternally seeking us to save us, and if we turn to Him when depression threatens to render life meaningless and pointless, too heavy a burden to carry, He will lift us out of this state. Sometimes, God heals with astonishing rapidity, miraculously, as it were. But most of the time, healing is a long journey in which we come to know God better, and as we know Him better, we understand ourselves better, as well.

Daily Reflection and Meditation
Dejection

Have you ever considered depression or dejection to be sinful? Why or why not?

_____
_____
_____
_____
_____

Think back over your life and remember struggles with depression, including currently ones. Ask your Father how He could have or can now help you. Record your answer.

_____
_____
_____
_____
_____

Ask the Holy Spirit to show you ways in which you are hopeless, places in your life or in your heart that you do not really believe God can heal or repair.

_____
_____
_____
_____

How would you live differently if your hope in Jesus Christ could not fail?

Listlessness

Listlessness is frequently associated with depression. It is, at least as defined contemporarily, a lack of energy or interest in activities around us, and a sense of apathy about life in general. Again, this is not something we think of as a sin, but as more of a condition. If we contrast our own lives with the life of Christ, we can see that He never lacked interest in what was going on around Him, nor was He ever apathetic about people or situations. Christ was vibrantly alive, filled with divine life, and thoroughly engaged in living while He was on this earth. In this comparison it is easier for us to see listlessness as sin: it keeps us from growing in Christ and Christian life and prevents us from being fully alive.

But listlessness also has another meaning as it has been used over the centuries. Listlessness refers to laziness. In fact, some writers describing the mortal sins refer to this sin as sloth, specifically meaning an unwillingness to work or exert oneself. This is more widely seen and is independent of depression. It is important to remember that the identification of deadly or cardinal sins originated out of monastic communities. Individuals with certain behaviors and attitudes matured in Christian life and bore the fruit of the Spirit, while others with the opposite behaviors and attitudes did not. Moreover, the latter group actually exhibited a lessening of their passion for and commitment to Jesus Christ, hence, "mortal" sins. These sins were deadly to faith. In the context of a monastery, laziness would have been obvious. Monastic communities live, eat, work, and pray together. Long before Muslims were praying five times each day, Christians were praying eight times every day, approximately every three hours, including Matins at three a.m. Work was a form of discipline that staved off sin. Being busy accomplishing specific, assigned tasks occupied the body and kept monks from being idle.[12] As early as the twelfth or thirteenth century, the phrase "idleness is the devil's

---

[12] For this reason, many monasteries have become known over the centuries for particular goods or products. Icons were originally made in monastic communities and continue to be so on Mt. Athos. Champagne was first bottled in a monastic community in France. Before the printing press, virtually every Bible was hand copied by monks. Monasteries are self-supporting, growing their own food, and selling goods and/or religious items – handmade crosses or candles, for example – to generate additional income to provide necessities for the monastery.

workshop," was floating around. The saying is commonly thought to be found in writing first in Chaucer's "Tale of Melibee," circa 1386, [13] and was phrased "Idle hands are the devil's tool." One has only to think of unsupervised children after school. When my siblings and I were adolescents and/or early teens, my mother went to work. Each day, she left specific chores for us to do after we rode the bus home from school. We knew exactly how much time was needed to perform the assigned duties, and virtually every shenanigan we pulled during our youth occurred after our chores were completed while our parents were at work.

Paul wrote:

> In the name of the Lord Jesus Christ, we command you, brothers, to keep away from every brother who is idle and does not live according to the teaching you received from us. For you yourselves know how you ought to follow our example. We were not idle when we were with you, nor did we eat anyone's food without paying for it. On the contrary, we worked night and day, laboring and toiling so that we would not be a burden to any of you. We did this, not because we do not have the right to such help, but in order to make ourselves a model for you to follow. For even when we were with you, we gave you this rule: 'If a man will not work, he shall not eat.'
>
> We hear that some among you are idle. They are not busy; they are busybodies. Such people we command and urge in the Lord Jesus Christ to settle down and earn the bread they eat. And as for you, brothers, never tire of doing what is right.[14]

Laziness implies that others are required to do for us what we are able to do for ourselves. It is a form of selfishness and self-indulgence, both of which are antithetical to growth in Christian life. One cannot grow in selflessness while at the same time expecting others to provide for him or her and take care of one's own responsibilities. At the same time, work is both humbling and edifying. Accomplishing something productive is rewarding and fulfilling at the end of the day. Work is a form of giving back to the world that sustains us. Although most of us no longer live in environments that allow a person to be

---

[13] Geoffrey Chaucer, *Canterbury Tales*.
[14] 2 Thessalonians 3:6-13.

self-sustaining, adding back to the total value of society's good in some form of work is good for us spiritually.

As of this writing, the unemployment rate in the United States is below 4%.[15] Unemployment fluctuates from year to year, but over the decades in which it has been measured, the current unemployment rate is the lowest ever recorded and indicates a strong desire among U.S. citizens to be gainfully employed.[16] In some degree, laziness is encouraged in our society in the name of recreation. Early in the twentieth century when labor unions became a strong influence in the workplace following the industrial revolution, one of the arguments for a shortened workweek was the benefit of free time. People would be able to enjoy some of the finer aspects of human creativity. Reading classical literature or studying renowned artwork were suggested as benefits for recreational use of time, as well as the cultivation of hobbies such as individual art or music. While perhaps that might have been the case in the lives of some individuals, the *de facto* outcome of recreational time for the enhancement of workers became entertainment.[17] America may be the most "entertained" society in the world. It is hard to argue that we are culturally improved for the number of hours we spend watching television, going to the movies, or, as has become common in the last twenty or so years, surfing the internet. We do indeed gain information, but the usefulness of that information is often dubious at best.

In a monastery idleness and laziness would have been much more obvious than it is in our society. Yet, time wasted is still time wasted in whatever century we happen to live. In our spare time we are not mastering new skills for the most part. We are being entertained. Hobbies can be productive means of adding to society without associated income, time spent in learning new

---

[15] US Department of Labor, Bureau of Labor, October 4, 2019.

[16] A simple reminder here: prior to the second World War and the era of the Depression, a great many families were self-supporting on small farms or through the provision of services in rural areas. Unemployment statistics were not compiled nationally until 1948 in the post-WWII economy. The Department of Labor, as a Cabinet level department, did not exist until 1913. Such was the impact of the rural and agricultural state of national employment prior to the industrial revolution and the World Wars.

[17] The labor unions of the time could not possibly have imagined the advent of television and computer and their impact on society.

skills, or in utilizing skills possessed such as carpentry, quilting, growing and canning food, and many more. According to the Bureau of Labor Statistics, those who work spend an average of less than six-and-a-half hours per weekday working and an average of about four hours per day in leisure activity, not including sleeping, eating, housekeeping, shopping, and more.[18] When we as a nation spend a quarter of a twenty-four hour day working, it is reasonable to suggest that we are inclined toward idleness. Statistics are only a general picture and do not speak to any single individual's work ethic, but they are revealing regarding the values of the nation as a whole.

My point is simply this: there is more laziness in our lives than we are likely to recognize. Recreation and "down time" are virtues in our society, and while some of both are necessary for physical and psychological regeneration, we probably have more of both in our lives than we actually need. From a purely Christian perspective, restoration and relaxation occur during sleep, not play. Laziness is a deadly vice because it gives us the opportunity to engage in activities we might not have chosen if we had been otherwise occupied. The spare time of a Christian ought to be utilized in prayer, meditation on Scripture, and ministry to others. If judgment day is the occasion on which we see the person we might have been in Jesus Christ in comparison to the person we chose to be, the impact of the time we wasted in this life will be acutely obvious and equally disappointing.

To combat laziness, we first have to agree that it is a sin. Doing so, we then need to evaluate our usage of time and decide what portion is spent in idleness. It would be interesting to know what God considers lazy as opposed to what we consider lazy. Spending time in prayer seeking the discernment of the Spirit is a good place to start. With the aid of the Holy Spirit, we can struggle against laziness through prayer and the intentional effort to avoid those activities that waste time. As mentioned above, we should study and meditate upon Scripture. This allows us to spend time growing in Christ rather than simply wasting time on something we will not remember a week from now. We need to have patience when we are tempted toward idleness and be intentional about struggling against it. The listlessness of depression is similar. Regardless of how we feel, we should strive to get up and do something. That *something* will

---

[18] https://www.bls.gov/charts/american-time-use/activity-by-emp.htm, October 2019.

have even more impact if we are doing something for someone else. Most depression is eased by activity, which turns our thoughts outward in even the most mundane activities. When we are listless, inactivity compounds the depression, which in turn increases listlessness and usually isolation, thus creating a deepening spiral of depression. God can and will heal us if we continue to seek Him and choose to get up and do something productive instead of simply succumbing to the desire to do nothing.

Daily Reflection and Meditation
Listlessness

Do you believe idleness is a sin? Why or why not?

_____
_____
_____
_____
_____

Ask the Holy Spirit to show you laziness in your own life. What do you see?

_____
_____
_____
_____
_____

What might you accomplish if you did not waste time?

_____
_____
_____
_____
_____

Compare and contrast wasting time with wasting life. How do your findings relate to your life?

_____
_____
_____
_____
_____
_____

Self-Esteem

This is the great American virtue heralded in every quarter of society as the most needed quality for… For what? Esteeming oneself has not proven to form a hard worker. To the contrary, the encouragement of self-esteem in our society has produced a generation of people who tend to think they have accomplished a great deal simply by doing the job for which they are paid. Children who have never lost or failed are ill-prepared for adulthood and expect to receive accolades for mediocrity because excellence was never considered or sought. Self-esteem is a quality that involves a sense of one's own worth, a regard for and pride in self, and the assumption of respect for oneself. The problem is that self-esteem for self-esteem's sake is based on nothing. If one has done nothing respectable or dignified, why should one have a high self-esteem?

When my grandson was a teenager, he failed in an endeavor he had undertaken and was terribly disappointed. When I spoke with his mother, she assured me she had had several long conversations with him because this had been a blow to his self-esteem, and she wanted to build up his self-confidence again. My own reaction was significantly different. When he came to me, our conversation included the many ways in which he had not put forth the necessary effort and was personally responsible for the failure. If he wanted to succeed in his next endeavor – indeed, any endeavor – then he would have to work harder than he did on that one. I assured him that he was more than capable of accomplishing what he wants, but being capable and actually doing what is required are two very different matters. His mother was not especially pleased with me, but this illustrates the point I want to make about self-esteem. Self-esteem without any basis in reality is nothing other than undue pride in oneself and unmerited high opinion of self. When my grandson pointed out that I was "making him feel badly about himself," I responded that he probably should feel badly about himself in this situation. He had not respected himself enough to do the work that was necessary and therefore failed. He had a legitimate reason for being disappointed in himself. After an extended conversation on self-respect and personal responsibility over the course of a couple of days, I offered him a means to redeem himself and have a second opportunity to succeed, which he undertook with only a modicum of long-term success.

Our efforts to encourage self-esteem in our children, however well-intentioned, might be more effective if we encouraged self-respect. For those children who live in an environment in which they are valued little or not at all, self-respect would accomplish the same outcome of establishing worth, but it would be based on what the child can do and the potential she possesses as opposed to the fact that the child was simply born. Children are not blind. They know who is smart and who works hard and who fails.

Self-esteem as a deadly sin is more insidious than what we are doing to our children. St. John Cassian's understanding of self-esteem was broader and included elements present in all of us. If we assess our heart and mind fairly, we will discover that each of us possesses some of these traits, usually in large doses. When we do things to please people rather than God or to be admired for our faithfulness, we are feeding our sense of self and self-importance. The desire for worldly approval is directly related to the issue of self-esteem: our sense of worth is derived from human beings, not from God. Attempting to impress others, either in a worldly sense or a hyper-spiritual manner, is a false form of self-affirmation and esteem of self. So much of what we value as a society encourages self-esteem that is damaging to our relationship with God. Seeking youthfulness, glamour, praise, and acclaim are all obstacles to being truly Christ-like. Nothing in His character or behavior indicated an interest in worldly approval in any form.

We esteem ourselves too highly or too much when we are pleased with the works we do for God. Working with Christ for the good of others is rewarding, and we can enjoy that. However, righteous works are a natural response to the love and grace we have received from God and are done in and through the indwelling of the Holy Spirit. For these works, we cannot claim credit even if we enjoy what we are doing. That is the point Paul was making when he wrote, "For by the grace given me I say to every one of you: Do not think of yourself more highly than you ought, but rather think of yourself with sober judgment, in accordance with the measure of faith God has given you."[19] The best in each of us was not only given to us in our creation, it was brought out by the work of the Holy Spirit in us. We reach full humanity only when we are totally dependent upon God, which is the natural state of all creation.

---

[19] Romans 12:3.

We are healed of the sin of self-esteem when we seek God and His reward, not praise from others or even ourselves. When we consider who we are and what we accomplish, we need to compare ourselves to God, not to other people. We may or may not do more or behave better than others, but the standard for Christ-like living is Christ Himself. By His life and His heart and soul, we judge our accomplishments, both spiritual and physical.

The best antidote to self-esteem is given to us by Paul in his letter to Philippi, "Your attitude should be the same as that of Christ Jesus: Who, being in very nature God, did not consider equality with God something to be grasped, but made Himself nothing, taking the very nature of a Servant, being made in human likeness."[20] If the Son of God could take on the nature of a servant and be content, then by the transforming power of the Holy Spirit, so can we.

---

[20] Philippians 2:5-7.

Daily Reflection and Meditation
Self-Esteem

Prior to reading this chapter, what was your opinion of self-esteem, and how was that opinion formed?

_____
_____
_____
_____
_____

What do you believe is the correct view of self-esteem and why?

_____
_____
_____
_____
_____

Describe in your own words the difference between self-esteem and self-respect.

_____
_____
_____
_____
_____

Can you think of any biblical examples in which Jesus sought or expressed self-esteem? If so, what are those?

_____
_____
_____
_____
_____
_____

Pride

Of the mortal sins, pride is the deadliest of all. If we were able to eradicate pride, the Spirit would be free to heal us of all the rest of the sins that harm our fellowship with God. But pride is pervasive and deep. It corrupts the whole soul and darkens it completely leading to our downfall. Pride was first seen in the Archangel Lucifer, the beautiful angel with a heavenly status equal to that of the Archangel Michael. The fall of Lucifer was a result of his pride and is described by Isaiah, including his ultimate fate.

> How you have fallen from heaven, O morning star, son of the dawn! You have been cast down to the earth, you who once laid low the nations! You said in your heart, 'I will ascend to heaven; I will raise my throne above the stars of God; I will sit enthroned on the mount of assembly, on the utmost heights of the sacred mountain. I will ascend above the tops of the clouds; I will make myself like the Most High.' But you are brought down to the grave, to the depths of the pit. Those who see you stare at you, they ponder your fate: 'Is this the man who shook the earth and made kingdoms tremble, the man who made the world a desert, who overthrew its cities and would not let his captives go home?'[21]

The original sin of humanity is typically identified as pride because the sin was the desire to attain equality with God – complete knowledge and therefore control and power – apart from God. It takes a great deal of pride to try to be God, but we do it all the time. When we believe our ways of doing things and making choices are wiser than God's, we are proud. When we seek to control events and manipulate outcomes, we are proud. When we try to accomplish our plans and purposes rather than God's, we are proud. When we do good things by His grace and through the Holy Spirit, but do not give God credit, we are proud. Pride arises all the time, and it is always destructive. It is especially dangerous for us when we begin to reflect Christ and exhibit a measure of grace and godliness, then begin to think we have achieved something, be it a measure of holiness or wisdom or righteousness. Paul's words to the church in Corinth need to be ever-present in our minds. "For who

---

[21] Isaiah 14:12-17.

makes you different from anyone else? What do you have that you did not receive? And if you did receive it, why do you boast as though you did not?"[22]

We have no cause for pride. Our true worth is discovered not in who we are or by anything we do, but in the words of Holy Communion. "The Body of Christ is broken for you, and the Blood of Christ is shed for you." There can be no greater value than that bestowed by the love of God expressed for us in the sacrifice of His Son on our behalf. He created us; He gave us life; He bestowed gifts and talents upon us, and then He gave His whole Self to save us from ourselves. Of what do we have to be proud? If we are going to be proud, then let it be of the magnificent and wondrous God Who loves the world so much He gave His Son to save it. Even Jesus said, "'Why do you call Me good?' Jesus answered. 'No one is good – except God alone.'"[23]

The obvious solution to pride is humility, but humility does not come easily for us. With the help of the Holy Spirit, humility grows in us through faith, fear of God, gentleness, and ridding ourselves of excess. Just about the time we realize we are humble, we commend ourselves on this spiritual accomplishment, and pride swells within us.

To be Christian is to be like Christ. That sounds reasonable until we take a serious look at Who He is. We talk about the sinful nature, and in broad terms, it appears to be something we can address. Even when we understand the sinful nature cannot be overcome without the work of the Spirit within us, we do not realize the gravity, depth, and permeating reach of sin in us. We are indeed a long way from being like Christ. When we search our soul and see what is truly there, we can and should be disheartened by what we discover there. As C.S. Lewis observed after taking his first long look at his own soul, "For the first time I examined myself with a seriously practical purpose. And there I found

---

[22] 1 Corinthians 4:7.

[23] Mark 10:18. Jesus' remarks were made in response to a man's desire to know how to inherit the Kingdom of God. The man lived a righteous life, following all the laws and commands of his Jewish heritage. Yet, following laws did not establish the man's goodness. Instead, Jesus commanded him to "sell everything he had and give it to the poor, then store up treasures in heaven by following Jesus." (v. 21) God is good, and we participate in that goodness when we treasure the things of heaven, first and foremost, God Himself. Jesus' statement is also an opaque reference to Who He really was: the Son of God, thus deserving the descriptive "good."

what appalled me: a zoo of lusts, a bedlam of ambitions, a nursery of fears, a harem of fondled hatreds. My name is legion."[24]

No longer is it common for us to examine ourselves closely. By normalizing human nature, we have normalized sin and therefore, think nothing of it. Recognizing sin for what it is, is daunting and often painful when realize the breadth of its scope and the depth of its weave within us. Yet, when we talk about being released from the sinful nature, we are talking about these sins, the mortal vices that lead us away from God and toward death. Not only do we accept these sins as a normal part of human nature, we even consider several to be a healthy part of our nature. What we must come to understand is that these sins are indeed deadly to the life God gives through His Spirit. The fallen human nature from which Christ came to save us is exactly what is normal to us.

We do not have to live bound by the legion of demons[25] to which Lewis referred. By the grace of God and the transformation of the Holy Spirit, the power of these sins over us can be defeated. We must agree to work with the Spirit and submit to His sometimes-painful healing process, but our Father's desire is to set us free from sin. To be sure, a measure of humility is in order. None of us will ever fully be free of these sins as long as we live in these clay vessels. And, perhaps that is the best reason to learn about and to revisit the deadly sins repeatedly throughout our lives – for the measure of humility given us when we discover them ever anew in our lives. Seeing for ourselves the depth of our need for salvation will increase our gratitude that our God loves so deeply and so completely that He freely offers salvation to us; first, on the Cross, second, throughout our lives as His Spirit works in us, and finally, on the last day when He raises us up and His creation is made new.

The new creation we became in our Baptism will slowly transform and become more like Christ as long as we continue to seek Him in humility. One day, His glory will be revealed in us, and we will discover that His plans for us and His work in us were greater than we ever imagined possible. Until then, we are wise to remember: every good thing comes from God.[26]

---

[24] C.S. Lewis, *Surprised by Joy* (New York: Harcourt Inc., 1955) 226.
[25] cf. Mark 5:9.
[26] cf. James 1:17.

Daily Reflection and Meditation
Pride

Of what accomplishment in your own life are you most proud, and why?
_____
_____
_____
_____
_____

What pride do you see in Jesus Christ?
_____
_____
_____
_____
_____

Ask the Holy Spirit to show you some of the pride in yourself. Record what you see.
_____
_____
_____
_____
_____

Paul wrote, "For it is by grace you have been saved – through faith and this not from yourselves, it is the gift of God – not by works, so that no one can boast. For we are God's workmanship, created in Christ Jesus to do good works, which God prepared in advance for us to do."[27] In light of the last two chapters on deadly sins, what do his words mean to you?

_____

_____

_____

_____

_____

_____

---

[27] Ephesians 2: 8-10.

VI

The Darkness Before the Dawn[*]

> "God whispers to us in our pleasures, speaks to us in our conscience, but shouts in our pains:
> it is His megaphone to rouse a deaf world."
> C.S. Lewis[1]

Of all the challenges to Christianity, perhaps the most influential of our generation is human suffering. If God is good, why is there suffering in the world? Not merely suffering, but intense, universal, inexplicable suffering comes in countless forms. We are a people seeking lives of pleasure with happy endings. But unbidden and almost always unexpected, suffering is visited upon every human life. Human instinct runs from such pain, and in a culture inebriated with entertainment, there is no longer any real understanding of or value in the fact of human suffering. We rebel against suffering in our lives, whisper well-meant platitudes to family and friends who suffer, and simply close our eyes to the vast human suffering beyond our capacity to assist. Yet, human suffering is a necessary and inevitable part of coming to know God. It is in the failure of this life and this world to satisfy and satiate that we turn toward the One Who is beyond.

Natural Suffering

Of all the forms in which suffering arises, nothing is more offensive than the apparent randomness of natural suffering – disease, death, and the uncontrollable outbursts of nature: hurricanes, volcanoes, tornados, droughts, floods, and the like. As frustrating as is the answer, this form of suffering is the easiest to explain. We live in a fallen world. The violation we experience in response to natural suffering is seldom eased by the inescapable fact of its existence, and however simple is the answer, it is most often the hardest to

---

[*] This chapter is an approximate synopsis of an as yet unpublished book *He Gave Up His Spirit* by the same author.
[1] C.S. Lewis, *The Problem of Pain* (New York: Harper Collins, 2001)

accept. Standing at the bedside of child consumed with cancer, stating the obvious that everybody dies is of little consolation if not outright offensive. But it is true. Everybody dies.

Human beings are the crown of creation,[2] alone made in the Image of God. When human beings fell from grace, so also did creation fall because creation is subject to the creature that has dominion over it. In Paul's letter to Rome, he wrote, "The creation waits in eager expectation for the sons of God to be revealed. For the creation was subjected to frustration, not by its own choice, but by the will of the one who subjected it, in hope that the creation itself will be liberated from its bondage to decay and brought into the glorious freedom of the children of God."[3] One day, this creation will be restored and perfected to all that God intends. The words of the Revelation, "He who was seated on the throne said, "I am making everything new!"[4] Then He said, "Write this down, for these words are trustworthy and true," apply not only to humanity but also to the whole of creation.

Until that time, our natural world is faulty and fails. Bodies are born with the seeds of death that eventually sprout, sometimes tragically sooner rather than later. Cataclysmic natural disasters strike with regularity. Through it all pass generations of human beings around the globe. Nameless faces of countless billions of lives fade into history. Such is the destiny awaiting us all, were it not for the Creator Who knew us before we born, has counted the hairs on our head, and loves us with an everlasting and infinite love. No human being ever came into existence who was not met by the love of God, even if His love was never known.

---

[2] This is the specifically Christian view of human beings. Many competing opinions about the place and value of human life exist in our world. Even in the twenty-first century, too many world leaders see human beings as a "renewable resource," and individual life holds little value. Some environmentalists go so far as to see human beings as the enemy of creation, rather than its king. At a "Planet Under Pressure" conference held in London, Professor Kari Norgaard of the University of Oregon presented a paper arguing that human beings should be packed more densely into population centers for the purpose of leaving nature undisturbed by human contact.
[3] Romans 8:19-21.
[4] Revelation 21:5.

When we face natural suffering, this is our consolation. Our Father knows our griefs, will sustain us in the greatest of misery, and has proven He will prevail through the Resurrection. This is all that Christians need know and speak when faced with the harsh reality of natural suffering. There is no easy answer. Suffering simply is, but the God of all creation will not fail to uphold us, comfort us, and walk with us in our darkest hours until He leads us into the light of His life.

C.S. Lewis could speak of the shout of God to us in our pain because, unless and until we experience the pain of this mortal life, we will not raise our hearts and minds to cry for help. Though in the end, God has given us triumph over life's sorrows and heartbreaks through Jesus Christ, His love for us will not allow suffering to be eradicated until the end of the age. God's desire is for us to know Him, and the pleasantry and satisfaction of the creation He has given us hide His presence until creation proves itself untrustworthy. The goal we need to set before us is attachment to the Triune God and detachment from the world. The deeper our fellowship with Jesus Christ, the freer we are both to enjoy life when it is good and to be patient and persevere in times of grief and pain.

Daily Reflection and Meditation
Natural Suffering

With the help of the Holy Spirit, reflect on your life and the tragedies that have occurred. In what ways did you blame God, and in what ways did you seek God?

_____
_____
_____
_____
_____
_____

How is your faith expressed in times of suffering? What does your response to suffering reveal about your faith in God?

_____
_____
_____
_____
_____
_____

What wounds from suffering in your life remain unhealed? What would be required for you to be healed?

_____
_____
_____
_____

The Darkness before the Dawn

_____

_____

Where is Christ in the midst of your suffering?

_____

_____

_____

_____

_____

_____

The Suffering of Sin

Far away and above, the most frequent source of misery in our lives is self-inflicted, almost exclusively unintentionally, but the inescapable result of our sinful nature. The motives that drive us, the fears that haunt us, the needs that starve us, all and more are the source of decisions and actions that have lifelong consequences, some of which cause deep suffering in our lives. The sinful nature has been considered at length, and the effects of that nature shape and form much of who we are today. In opportunities we ignored out of fear, in choices we made without a thought of Christ, in broken relationships and wounded feelings, the ways in which our own sin creates pain for us are as varied and numerous as are human beings and the complexities of the heart, mind, and soul.

Obvious examples would be things like driving drunk and causing an accident, harming or killing others, or ending a marriage simply because it is too much work to love another. More subtle examples include choices such as refusing to take a step for fear of the unknown or wishing to be and acting as if we are someone we are not. There is an endless array of ways in which the sinful nature expresses itself, and the vast majority of our suffering originates within us. When we look backward at our history, our inclination is to think that our environment and our relationships produced an often-impossible obstacle to becoming any better than we turned out to be, but this is unfair. Every human life is equally trapped by the sin that perverts, pollutes, and destroys us.

Daily we need to be reminded of Paul's words to Timothy, "Here is a trustworthy saying that deserves full acceptance: Christ Jesus came into the world to save sinners – of whom I am the worst."[5] An honest assessment of our lives and our choices reveals that we are the cause of most of our own suffering, and as such, we are the ones who most need a Savior. It does not matter from where we came or the circumstances of our past, we are the ones who, for whatever reasons, made the decisions that brought us to the point of pain. Consider, for example, that Jesus' parents were by no means without

---

[5] 1 Timothy 1:15.

fault,[6] nor was His upbringing one of privilege or perfection. Yet, Jesus' sinlessness and perfect obedience never caused Him to bring suffering upon Himself in the ways in which we do. If we had been perfectly obedient to our Father – or even tacitly obedient to Him – in our childhood and youth, a great many of the choices we made would have been different. That we did not know better or have a relationship with God does not make us less culpable; it merely reinforces our need to be saved.

Accepting the inevitability of our sinfulness instills a needed measure of humility in us, although it does not give us permission to continue blithely in sin. We are new creations in Christ Jesus, and we are called to be like Him. The offer of new life and a fresh start in Jesus Christ are ever-present. Even in faithfulness, we will still succumb to the sinful nature and make decisions that bring suffering to us and to others. The great promise of God's love is that in His providence, He will bring forth good in all things,[7] including our sinfulness. That is amazing, but that is our Father. His creative capacity to save and redeem are beyond anything we can fathom, and the worst of our suffering can be the source of good if we continually bring our failures and shortcomings to Him in repentance and supplication.

---

[6] Obviously, Mary and Joseph both are examples of great faith and obedience, but that does not mean they were without sin. Only One was without sin, and that was by virtue of Who He truly was: the Son of God. However devout and pious Jesus' parents may have been, they too struggled with the sinful nature and could not possibly have lived without its effects expressed in their lives as in our own.

[7] cf. Romans 8:28.

Daily Meditation and Reflection
The Suffering of Sin

What is the worst mistake you ever made? How did you respond to it?

_____
_____
_____
_____
_____
_____

Were you seeking Christ when you made the mistake (or bad choice)? How has your current relationship with Christ impacted the decisions you make, if at all?

_____
_____
_____
_____
_____
_____

Make a list of unhealed and/or unforgiven regrets, disappointments, and personal failures from your past. Begin taking them to Christ one at a time, asking for forgiveness and freedom and the healing and new life of the Spirit in each case.

_____
_____
_____
_____

Where is Christ is the midst of your suffering?

Freely You Have Received, Now Freely Give[8]

I really believe that everyone is doing the best he can do. The problem is that our best is sometimes quite awful. But every person makes the best decision she can make with the information she has at the time toward the outcome with the greatest perceived good. Apart from the indwelling and guidance of the Holy Spirit, we cannot possibly have sufficient information to make the best decision for the highest and truest good. Looking back at circumstances and events, people and decisions, can be informative, but beyond the wisdom gained, there is no helpful reason to hold onto the pain.

The sin of others is a frequent source of suffering for us. The multitudinous expression of the sinful nature in others wounds us through malice, envy, lies, rejection, pettiness, and the list goes on. The actions of others can create enormous pain in our lives, much as our own sin creates suffering in the lives of those we love and those we do not even know. When someone hurts us deeply, that wound can become a trophy of injustice we carry, eliciting sympathy and admiration for our forbearance in the face of wrongful suffering. Worse, however, are the spiritual and psychological effects of keeping a list of inflicted injuries in our hearts and minds. These breed bitterness, anger, and discontent within us, thus forming an ever-increasing obstacle between Christ and us.

The reason we cannot enjoy full fellowship with God when we cling to the sins of others against us is primarily because we are refusing to be like Christ and thus cannot grow as a Christian. Our sin is removed by His forgiveness, and to hold onto the sins of others is a rejection of all that He has done for us. When we refuse to forgive others, we become like the man in Jesus' parable[9] who was forgiven a debt of ten thousand talents but refused to forgive a debt of one hundred denarii. The forgiven but unforgiving man was thrown in prison and tortured until his debt could be repaid. Jesus concludes with the statement, "This is how my heavenly Father will treat each of you unless you forgive your brother from your heart."[10] These are harsh words, but they echo the words of the Lord's Prayer, "Forgive us our debts, as we also have forgiven

---

[8] Matthew 10:8.
[9] cf. Matthew 18:23-35.
[10] ibid.

our debtors."[11] We are not given the option not to forgive and to harbor our treasured grudges. If we consider what it cost our Father to forgive us and the incalculable gift of His own Spirit that He eagerly gives us when we ask, by what unjust pride do we fail to forgive others?

It is easy enough to be forgiving toward those actions that cost us little, but it is far harder to forgive those that change the course of our lives. Yet, that is precisely what is expected of us. We did not ask for forgiveness when God made it available to us, and in the same way, we are to forgive before it is sought from us regardless of how deeply we are hurt and undeserved is the forgiveness. Our forgiveness in Jesus Christ is undeserved as well. To forgive outrageous sins against us demands deep and abiding trust in God. First, we must be truly convinced that He is able to redeem our lives from the pit, even the pit of another's making, and second, we must rely fully upon His ability to heal our hearts and minds from the harm inflicted. When someone has seriously sinned against us, we need the grace of Christ's healing Spirit to sustain us. It is a hard thing, sometimes almost unbearable, to bear the brunt of another person's sin. How well our Father knows this! He is compassionate toward our wounds and quick to respond generously when we call. The justice we receive for another's sin is the boundless love and healing of Jesus Christ. This is the far richer blessing than vengeance, even if we suppose retribution actually can satisfy our pain.

The world is fallen and held captive to sin and death. We cannot escape that reality. Just as sin is present in us, so also is it present in others. Seldom do people intend to hurt or harm someone else, but that is what sin does. When we grieve some sin against us, we are wise to remember the depth of pain because that is what we inflict on others in our sin. In the morass of human sin that threatens to stagnate our life in Christ through suffering, forgiveness is the gift that lifts both parties – the offended and the offender. Jesus Christ bought our forgiveness with His Cross, and when we choose to forgive, we are giving God the opportunity to bring a resurrection to our lives in the middle of our living. Forgiveness is costly, but resurrection is wondrous beyond expectation.

---

[11] Matthew 6:12.

Daily Reflection and Meditation

Freely You Have Received, Now Freely Give

Make a list of the people who have sinned against you and inflicted wounds on you. Include the sin by the name of the person who hurt you.

_____
_____
_____
_____
_____

Go through your list, and for each sin against you, write the consequences in your life. How did this sin actually hurt you, even if it was only your ego? What harm was done to you?

_____
_____
_____
_____
_____

One at a time, ask the Holy Spirit to reveal to you whether you have truly forgiven this person. If you have not, why not? How do you explain to Jesus Christ that you want His forgiveness while you choose not to forgive another?

_____
_____
_____

_____

_____

Each day, work through your list one at a time, asking for the determination and strength to forgive the person with the whole of your heart.

_____

_____

_____

_____

_____

_____

Christian Suffering

Up to this point, we have considered suffering experienced by every human being who has ever lived. The value of suffering is its revelation of our need for God. Whether in the form of the sin of creation – natural suffering – or human sin, everyone suffers, and we are blessed by suffering when we turn to God for help. Yet, one form of suffering unique to faithful disciples remains. "Blessed are you when people insult you, persecute you and falsely say all kinds of evil against you because of Me. Rejoice and be glad, because great is your reward in heaven, for in the same way they persecuted the prophets who were before you."[12]

We live in a world that crucified the Son of God, and this generation is not different in nature than the generation in which Jesus lived. If we are truly faithful to Jesus Christ, we will change, and as we change, not everyone we know will be happy about it. The goal of life in Christ is transformation, to become ourselves and to be truly alive as christs in the world, living icons of our God. Jesus said, "If the world hates you, keep in mind that it hated Me first. If you belonged to the world, it would love you as its own. As it is, you do not belong to the world, but I have chosen you out of the world. That is why the world hates you. Remember the words I spoke to you: 'No servant is greater than his Master.' If they persecuted Me, they will persecute you also. If they obeyed My teaching, they will obey yours also. They will treat you this way because of My Name, for they do not know the One who sent Me."[13]

There are many people in the world who oppose Christianity. These people are our mission field; these are the ones we are called to love and called to offer salvation through Jesus Christ. If we are true to Him, the day will come when we will be persecuted for His Name's sake. Someone somewhere will punish us for being Christian, if we are sufficiently Christ-like. At that moment we will want to lash out, for we have sought *their* good and *their* blessing, and in return, we have been struck down. Do not be deceived: it is hard to rejoice because we have joined the league of the prophets before us. But we are not better than our Master, and we are not immune to the suffering He bore. We cannot receive the life He gives and be unwilling to follow in His footsteps.

---

[12] Matthew 5:11-12.
[13] John 15:18-21.

His footsteps *lead* us to life, but on that journey, some will want us to stumble and fall. Of Jesus' original twelve disciples, only the Apostle John died of old age. The other eleven were martyred for their faith, often in horrible and painful ways.

Today in western Christianity, none of us face death for being a disciple of Jesus Christ, but we will face mockery, rejection, and persecution from time to time. However, what we face is nothing by comparison to Christians in other parts of the world. Christians in China simply disappear and are never seen again. The same is true in many Islamic countries. Christian faith is not tolerated. In those places where Christian faith is allowed but not sanctioned, Christians often live as second-class citizens, excluded from universities and professions, segregated from prominent society. There are some people in the United States today who encourage this type of treatment of Christians in America. Our nation continues to be increasingly polarized in intellectual and moral direction, and a huge factor in that deepening conflict of beliefs is religious faith in general and Christian faith specifically. Students educated in parochial schools or home-schooled children face significant hurdles getting into some of the better universities. Openly Christian employees are sometimes passed over for promotion because of their faith. The broader the acceptance of religion as a purely private moral matter, the more likely Christians are to encounter overt hostility in the course of their lifetime.

Knowing that some form of persecution, albeit not death for any of us, is inevitable at least prepares us somewhat when the time comes. I will say, however, that my observation is that we are never really prepared and are shocked when it happens. If we mean no ill will, then being greeted with antagonism and animosity comes as a surprise to most of us, in spite of the fact that we follow as crucified Lord. Likewise, as others before us have done, many of us will stumble in faith when we face some sort of persecution. If one is facing large tuition costs for the college education of children, for example, then minimizing or hiding devotion to Christ to get a higher paying position feels necessary. These are the sorts of ways in which we will be tempted to deny our relationship with Jesus Christ. Our God is a merciful God, and He knows what we need. However, the world will not always accommodate Christian faith, and because this is true, it falls to each of us to assess carefully in prayer the distinction between what we need and what we want. Such decisions have not been as obviously necessary in the past, but they will become more so in the future. We cannot have it all – everything the world offers, and total commitment to Jesus Christ. Eventually, the two will come into conflict. The decision we make will determine our witness to the value of Jesus Christ. If we choose Him over the world, others will want to know what is so valuable to us that we are willing to sacrifice worldly gain. Martyrdom had the opposite effect of squelching the early Christian community. It bore testimony to the enduring meaning and power of the life offered by the Christian God. The same is true today in countries where Christians are killed for their faith. In like manner our faithfulness at personal and temporal cost to us bears witness to the eternal value of knowing God, and thus, draws people to Him.

Suffering because we are like Christ is a mark of mature discipleship. We have been sufficiently transformed to be a threat to worldly values and worldly power. The devil has no reason to attack those who do nothing for the Kingdom of God. It is when we are effective apostles of Jesus Christ, going out into the world to bring the light and life of God into the darkness and death that pervade human existence that we draw the attention of evil. After all, Job's righteousness was the catalyst for his worldly downfall.[14] Moreover, it was God Himself Who drew attention to Job. So it is with us as well. As our lives become an increasing testimony to the transforming life and love of Jesus Christ, we will be lifted up as examples of faithfulness. This is necessary and right to draw people to Christ. God will want others to see Christ in and through us. Many will respond positively; Jesus attracted large crowds. But we also will draw the attention of both the evil one and those who oppose Christianity.

None of us actually wants to suffer, but suffering comes in every person's life. In the trials of suffering that all human beings experience, we are given the opportunity to see the beauty of God's providence, mercy, and provision. In all of our suffering, God is with us, even in the suffering we bring on ourselves. When the question of suffering is raised, the longing that underlies our expectation of a painless world reveals our confusion of this world with the Kingdom of God. This world will never be without suffering. Only when

---

[14] Job 1:1-12.

Christ comes in glory and makes all things new[15] will suffering come to an end. Until that great and glorious day, suffering is a tool of revelation, revealing the fallen and unsatisfactory nature of this world and the perfect goodness and life of the God and His Kingdom. In the midst of suffering, God calls us to Himself. As George MacDonald once said, "The Son of God suffered unto death, not that men might not suffer, but that their suffering might be like His."[16]

Redemptive.

---

[15] cf. Revelation 21:5, also the prophecy found in Isaiah 43:19.
[16] George MacDonald (1824-1905), Scottish minister, author, and poet, *Unspoken Sermon Series One:* The Consuming Fire.

Daily Reflection and Meditation

Christian Suffering

In what way have you understood suffering, whether in your life or in general?

_____
_____
_____
_____
_____

Most of us follow Jesus Christ for the rich blessings we receive. How ready are you to be persecuted for being a Christian?

_____
_____
_____
_____
_____

Does the idea of suffering for your faith make you more or less inclined to grow in Christian life? Explain your response.

_____
_____
_____
_____
_____

How can your personal suffering be redemptive for others?

_____
_____
_____
_____
_____
_____

VII

From Glory into Glory

And the Journey Goes On

Becoming a new creation in Jesus Christ is the first form of glory. We are participants in the divine nature,[1] partakers of the divine nature. In a mystical sense, the Spirit of Christ dwells within us, and the glory that belongs to the Father is shared with us. Given what we know of human nature, wisdom suggests that we not think too much of the glory given to us, lest we become impressed by the glory of God in a sinful and self-serving way – a way in which we are certain to obscure not only our relationship with Christ Jesus, but also the revelation of Him to others through us. This is the means by which we bear witness to Christ, less in what we say and do than in who we are because of Who He is in us.[2] Maturation in Christian life necessarily means the sinful nature is giving way to the virtues of the Divine nature through our obedience to the transforming work of the Spirit. This process begins and continues throughout our lives so that we might become ourselves, fully alive in Jesus Christ, and also so others might come to know Him through us.

St. Irenaeus wrote, "For the glory of God is a living man; and the life of man consists in beholding God. For if the manifestation of God which is made by means of the creation, affords life to all living in the earth, much more does that revelation of the Father which comes through the Word, give life to those who see Him."[3] First, St. Irenaeus speaks of a "living man." Here, he is not referring to life after death, but to living, breathing human beings in the here and now. The life we receive after death is the same eternal life given to us by

---

[1] cf. 2. Peter 1:4.

[2] This statement is not meant to imply that we are not called to speak and to do on behalf of Christ and to strive to draw others to Him. To the contrary, that is exactly what we are called to do: to take salvation in Jesus Christ to the ends of the earth. (cf. Acts 13.47) As stated earlier, however, our doing – and our saying – necessarily must flow first from our being in Christ.

[3] *Against Heresies, Ante-Nicene Fathers,* Volume 1, Book IV, eds. Alexander Roberts and James Donaldson (Peabody: Hendrickson Publishers, 1999) p. 490.

the Holy Spirit. The glory of God to which St. Irenaeus speaks is you and me. If God is to be seen and glorified on this earth, then it will be through His children, more specifically, through His children who have seen Him.

God is seen in creation – the manifestation of God – by the life He gives to all creation. In springtime it is not hard to behold God, to see the new life that bursts forth in rich and lush color, or in young calves and foals scampering close to their mothers, or in the romantic songs of birds calling to mate. Equally, God is made known in creation through the seasons, from the vibrancy of spring to the cold death of winter, the annual cycle of which mimics the cycle of human life. Nothing bespeaks the Resurrection more clearly than the dormant bulb of winter that bursts into life in the spring. The life that God gives creation reveals Him if we want to see. Yet, how much more is God revealed by those who are born of Christ and reach the stage of maturity in which they see Him!

In other words the stage of spiritual healing and maturation described as *theoria* refers to the revelation of the Father in Jesus Christ that gives life to those to whom the Father reveals Himself. Consider, for example, the impact of seeing God – not so much with physical eyes – although that is possible in a mystical manifestation, but with the eyes of the soul. The vision of God is transforming because the Object of our faith is now seen, and our hope becomes certainty. Such a transition from faith and hope to the vision of the Source of all love magnifies our longing for God and our devotion to Him. His greatness far exceeds anything our minds have imagined, and simply His Presence demands humility and gratitude from us. From this humility and gratitude, ever conscious of the distance between Creator and creature, our repugnance at sin and desire for virtue increase. From this heightened relationship with God, we are exponentially more alive, and the vitality of life both sheds glory into the creature and glorifies the Creator.

How this progression in spiritual healing and Christian maturation occurs is not entirely unknown to us, although most of us do not recognize the disclosure of this instruction even though we have seen it often and can sometimes recite it by heart. I am here referring to the Beatitudes found both in the Gospels according to Matthew and Luke,[4] given in the larger context of

---

[4] Matthew 5:1-12; Luke 6:17-23.

the Sermon on the Mount and the Sermon on the Plain, respectively. Most scholars assume these are two different versions of the same event, reported from variant memories. However, Jesus' Sermon on the Mount appears to be primarily for His disciples, reported as though they left the crowds behind, went up on the mount, and Jesus taught the disciples there.[5] In contrast, the Sermon on the Plain specifically mentions the crowds around Jesus.[6] Likewise, the content and count of the Beatitudes are slightly different, the Matthean account emphasizing the condition of the heart at length and the shortened Lukan version this earthly life. Instruction to the disciples was consistently more in-depth than were Jesus' sermons to the crowds, which perhaps accounts for the difference between the two sets of Beatitudes.

Robert Schuller's *Be (Happy) Attitudes*[7] is a practical, though reductionistic, interpretation of the Beatitudes, and Schuller's interpretation has done a great disservice to the meaning and beauty of the Beatitudes as taught in their original context by Jesus. What Jesus laid out in eight fairly simple statements is the necessary pathway of growth in virtue, i.e.: maturation in Christian life and faith. In contrast, Schuller's account of the Beatitudes is both worldly and self-serving, as compared to Jesus' practical application of the Beatitudes in Luke. From early on, great preachers and writers in Christianity[8] understood the Beatitudes as steps toward ever-increasing

---

[5] See Matthew 5:1-2, the reference is to the disciples distinct from the crowd.

[6] cf. Luke 6:17.

[7] Robert Schuller, Be (Happy) Attitudes (Irving: Word, Inc., 1987). The eight beatitudes, roughly translated, are as follows: "1. I need Help; I can't do it alone! 2. I'm really hurting but am going to bounce back. 3. I'm going to remain cool, calm and collected. 4. I really want to do the right thing. 5. I'm going to treat others the way I want them to treat me. 6. I've got to let faith flow freely through me. 7. I'm going to be a bridge builder. 8. I can choose to be happy, anyway!" This interpretation does not do justice even to the more simplistic instruction given in the Lukan account of the Beatitudes. Although highly popular and still in print after three decades, the *Be (Happy) Attitudes* are uniquely suited to late twentieth-century "feel good" Christianity of vacuous content. By comparison to the actual meaning of the Matthean Beatitudes, Schuller's *Be (Happy) Attitudes* borders on the absurd.

[8] Notably: Origen (b. 185, fl. c. 200-254); Hilary (c. 315-367); Jerome (c. 347-420); John Chrysostom (c. 344/354-407, fl. 386-407); Chromatius (fl. 400); Augustine (354-430); St. Symeon the New Theologian (949-1022); among others.

Christian life and virtue. It is that interpretation we need to recover and pursue in our own lives under the tutelage of the Holy Spirit.

Daily Reflection and Meditation
And the Journey Goes On

The great blessing of Christian faith is knowing God. That *is* the benefit of being a Christian. The more deeply we know Him, the more His glory is reflected through us to the world. What are obstacles in your life that keep you from living fully and hide the glory of God in you?

_____

_____

_____

_____

_____

Ask the Holy Spirit to help you answer the question above. Ask Him to show you what is the first obstacle He would like to remove so you may know God more fully and become His glory in the world. What did the Spirit bring to your mind?

_____

_____

_____

_____

_____

How willing are you to submit to release this particular attachment, habit, or value in order to be more alive in Jesus Christ?

_____

_____

Do you think Jesus Christ is revealed in you, and if so, to what extent? Do you understand your life as a tool of the revelation of Jesus Christ? Why or why not?

Poverty and Mourning

Poverty and mourning come with a set of preconceived, twenty-first century notions, some ambivalent and some negative. As with nearly everything in Christianity, the meaning of each is turned upside down in the Kingdom of God. The worldly negative becomes a spiritual positive, and poverty and mourning take on new meaning within the context of Jesus' teaching. *"Blessed are the poor in spirit..."*[9] Poverty of spirit is humility. Blessed are the humble. By far, I think humility is the most difficult of all virtues to attain. The moment we begin to think of ourselves as humble is also the moment pride begins to rise in us. The sin of the fall of Adam and Eve was the desire to be like God apart from God, to have equal knowledge as God, and is identified as pride. Pride comes in multitudinous forms – pride in our accomplishments is too obvious. More subtle forms of pride plague us in virtually every aspect of our lives: pride in our appearance, pride in our children, pride in our talents, pride in our suffering, pride in our Christian devotion, pride in our forgiveness of others, and the list goes on. Pride sneaks up within us every time we pat ourselves on the back for the good we have done or the patience we have shown.

Apart from the ones He gave us, we have no talents or skills. We do not even have life to claim as our own accomplishment, and that *is* the greatest gift. If we are beautiful by the world's standards, that is irrelevant to the God Who desires beauty of heart above all else. A man lost his son unexpectedly, and in his adjustment to this horrible reality came to understand that this death was his personal cross to bear. But surely, that is not true. The cross we bear is the same cross as Christ bore – the death of self to rise again and live for the salvation and redemption of others. Clinging to our suffering as a badge of faith is a form of pride. Christ carries our griefs and sorrows. The challenge, and thus the solution, is to remember that all true good within us comes from God, be it our best abilities or our faith in the time of suffering.

No pride is more dangerous and more insidious than pride in our goodness. If our desire is to grow in Christ and become more like Him, the day will come when we begin to sense our own spiritual maturity. Every one of us at one time or another will succumb to this form of pride with the best of intentions as we

---

[9] Matthew 5:3a.

do so. For that reason, it is better to know the pitfall that lies before us. If we mature as a Christian at all, that can only occur as a work of the Spirit. We choose to submit, but beyond that, every progression in spiritual life is given to us by God. Even in our submission, of what do we have to be proud? Submitting to the Lordship of God is merely accepting our rightful place before Him, and doing that very thing is often a continual challenge for us. The measure of our goodness is God Himself, and the measure of our value is His love. We are but a blip in the history of humankind, and the fact of our existence is pure gift. Humility calls us to this state of being, that of gratitude that our Creator gave us life, that His perfect goodness heals us, and that His love gives us infinite worth, just as His love gives everyone else the same eternal value.

As human beings, pride is the flip side of the same coin of insecurity and fear. Because there is much in us of which to be afraid and ashamed, we focus on that which seems good to us and take pleasure from the fact that we are not a totally lost cause. The greater our pride and/or arrogance, so also is the greater our insecurity and fear. They go hand in hand with one another. Yet, God despises all of these in our lives: pride, arrogance, insecurity, fear, and shame. All stand between us and the beauty and freedom of the saved and redeemed person God wants us to become. In *The Weight of Glory* C.S. Lewis wrote:

> And that is enough to raise your thoughts to what may happen when the redeemed soul, beyond all hope and nearly beyond belief, learns at last that she has pleased Him whom she was created to please. There will be no room for vanity then. She will be free from the miserable illusion that it is her doing. With no taint of what we should now call self-approval she will most innocently rejoice in the thing that God has made her to be, and the moment which heals her old inferiority complex forever will also drown her pride... Perfect humility dispenses with modesty.[10]

Humility is not an incessant drumbeat of self-flagellation. To the contrary, true humility is the fruit of our longing to please the Father we love, in response to His great love for us. When we become ourselves, we recognize this is our Father's doing, not our own. All that we thought we were, all that we took

---

[10] C.S. Lewis, *The Weight of Glory* (NY: Harper Collins, 2001), 37-38.

pride in being, gives way to a creature of nobility and majesty, one in whom we can delight because we are who God created us to be. No longer do we struggle with our fears and insecurities, but neither is there room for pride in ourselves. We are our Father's children, reflecting His glory and drawing life from Him.

The reward of the blessing of humility is the Kingdom of God. That is to say, to the extent that we are truly humble, we receive everything God wants to give. If we stopped right here at "poor in spirit," we would eventually grow in spite of ourselves, for in authentic humility of spirit, we truly become clay in the Potter's Hands.[11] There are no limits to God's desire to give us all that He has. He sent His Son to save us. He poured out His Spirit to give us eternal life. God wants us to be fully alive in Him and to receive every good thing He gives. As Jesus said, "Fear not, little flock, for it is your Father's good pleasure to give you the Kingdom."[12] Our Father takes pleasure in giving us all that He has. That is a monumental thought if we dare to trust it. Rather than striving and struggling for bits and pieces of life, our Father delights in giving us every good thing if we will run to Him as a little children[13] and receive from His Hand.

St. Symeon the New Theologian wrote:

> Where there is unfeigned humiliation there is also the depth of humility, and where there is humility, there is also the enlightenment of the Spirit. Where there is the enlightenment of the Spirit there is the outpouring of the light of God, there is God in the wisdom and knowledge of His mysteries. Where these mysteries are to be found, there is the Kingdom of heaven and the experience of the kingdom and the hidden treasures of the knowledge of God, which include the manifestation of poverty of spirit. Where poverty of spirit is perceived, there is also the sorrow that is full of joy. There are ever-flowing tears that purify the soul that loves these things and cause it to be completely filled with light.[14]

---

[11] cf. Isaiah 64:8.
[12] Luke 12:32 (RSV).
[13] cf. Mark 10:14.
[14] St. Symeon the New Theologian, *The Discourses*, CWS, (Mahwah, NJ: Paulist Press, 1980) 52-53.

"Blessed are those who mourn..."[15] The mourning of which Christ Jesus spoke was mourning for our sins, for our separation from God. When we do all we can to please God, we come to the realization that we cannot, for sin continues to plague us in spite of our best intentions. At the moment of recognition, holy mourning is the appropriate response. We need to be deeply grieved that we are not and indeed cannot attain the richness of soul for which we long because of our sin. St. Symeon attaches joy to the sorrow for sins – sorrow that leads to poverty of spirit, for this is the comfort we receive – joy! In our humiliation for our sinfulness, the treasures of the Kingdom of God are given to us. Rightfully, we can and should mourn for the state of our souls. How far we are from being like Christ!

It is important here to make a clarification. Jesus does *not* want us to mourn for the things of this world, to wallow in the grief of another's death, or to sorrow over daily losses. Paul wrote, "Godly sorrow brings repentance that leads to salvation and leaves no regret, but worldly sorrow brings death."[16] Worldly sorrow is grief for the things of this world: careers, position, fame, wealth, and even health and physical life. Everything in this life is transitory, for earthly life itself is temporary. Therefore, whatever our hopes, dreams, and successes, these too belong to this world. Some we will achieve; some we will lose. In the end, however, death conquers this life, and sorrow for this life brings death to our souls. Such sorrow reveals undue attachment to this life and this world.

Moreover, I am not suggesting that we not grieve when a loved one dies, but this type of grief is healed by the promise of the Resurrection. Death has given way to the victory of eternal life, and to sorrow to the point of despair is a denial of the Resurrection as definitive of our life and living. Both disease and death are simple facts of worldly life. To indulge in worldly sorrow detaches us from the hope and promise of the Resurrection and destroys the soul. Grief even for the loss of health and for death must be tempered by faith in the future God has in store for each of us.

The mourning about which St. Symeon wrote is a mourning for the riches of the Kingdom of God, and this is a legitimate question for each of us. Do we

---

[15] Matthew 5:4a.
[16] 2 Corinthians 7:10.

truly long for the Kingdom of God more than we long for the kingdom of this world? It is not possible to yearn for our Father's Kingdom if we are content with the physical world in which we live. We cannot grieve for what we do not have if we do not really want it.

Daily Reflection and Meditation

Poverty and Mourning

Do you desire the Kingdom of God more than you desire this world? Why or why not?

_____
_____
_____
_____
_____

Ask the Holy Spirit to show you your strongest unhealthy attachments to this world. Make a list of them as they come to mind.

_____
_____
_____
_____
_____

Why are these more valuable to you than Christ? What have they to offer that is more than what Christ is offering?

_____
_____
_____
_____
_____

Are you willing to accept the humiliation of soul necessary to receive what God wants to give you? Why or why not?

What is your greatest fear about choosing the life of Christ over the life of this world?

On the Heels of Poverty and Mourning[17]

"Blessed are the meek..."[18] Meek is not a common word in contemporary language, nor is it a particularly desirable trait, as we understand its meaning. Our tendency is to think of a meek person as a shy and timid individual, neither of which appear to be stellar reflections of Christ. Yet, the quality of meekness follows from humility and holy mourning. Becoming meek is the natural progression in spiritual life when we mourn our sins in poverty of spirit. In this sense, then, to be meek is not to be timid or easily pushed around, but rather, a spiritually meek person is without anger, vanity, or insecurity. Our Father comforts our godly sorrow, and what remains is a person detached from this world. Ironically, in our detachment we inherit all the best this world can give. When we are meek, we are free to enjoy this world with unbounded enthusiasm.

When we possess neither pride of self or loathing of self but draw our worth and value from the love of God, the effect is a diminishment of the conceit and fear that cause us to respond to the provocations of the world in anger and pride. If we pause and think about it, this makes perfect sense. Most of the wounds inflicted by others are wounds of pride, disrespect, and rejection – not all, but most. The reason others are able to hurt us is because we want and need their affirmation and acceptance. To be sure, we are created to love and be loved, but if our sense of self is defined by our Father and instilled in us through His Spirit, we can regret that we are rejected, but we are not wounded by it. Moreover, both pride and worldly respect no longer drive us because godly sorrow separates us from all this world values. When we are poor in spirit, it is not possible to wound our pride, for we have none. Mourning for our own sins gives us tremendous patience with the sins of others, even those sins that

---

[17] In the interest of full disclosure, I think it is only fair to admit that much of the following is what I truly am convinced is promised to us. Personally, I am so lacking in humility that neither poverty of spirit nor holy mourning is long sustained in my own life. In my experience there have been, perhaps, glimpses of the truth of the progression of the soul, but these are fleeting at best, if indeed they are at all. Yet, the immaturity of my faith and life – or that of anyone else's – is not just cause to abandon the pursuit of God. If anything, the recognition of spiritual immaturity ought to be a clarion call to prayer, holy sorrow, and humiliation so we too might receive all God wants to give us.

[18] Matthew 5:5a.

insinuate themselves into our daily living. If we can do no more than weep before God because we are helpless against sin, how can we be harsh with others for the sins that are also our own?

What makes this state bearable for us is the consolation of the Spirit, the outpouring of God's love and light into our lives. These are infinitely preferable to petty whims of our egos. Living in this way, we become meek – lacking anger, pride, self-concern, insecurity, jealousy, and the like. The meek soul does indeed inherit the earth. There are great earthly blessings in the enjoyment of this life and this world in a spiritually detached state. We are free to delight in the good and be patient with the bad. But only a meek person has the capacity for such enjoyment of life. Unless and until we are meek, our experience of this life and world will be marred by our vanities and fears. Life will be at least as much burden as it is enjoyment, and happiness inevitably will be fleeting. "Blessed are the meek, for they will inherit the earth." It is only too true. When we are meek, every good thing in this world is there for us to embrace and enjoy, unblemished by the surges of sin within us.

Poverty of spirit brings mourning for the confinement and restrictions of sin. This holy mourning is met by joy when we hunger for the life of the Kingdom – when we *"hunger and thirst for righteousness."*[19] The most fundamental fact of human existence is the need for food and water to sustain life. Jesus' use of the words *hunger* and *thirst* reflect the urgency with which we are to yearn for righteousness. God does not want us to strive to be righteous. Only God is righteous. When we hunger and thirst for righteousness, then we are hungering and thirsting for what God alone can give. The promise we receive is that we will be filled. But is that not the promise that has been given always – that God will give us His Spirit, His life? Jesus places this reward in the appropriate stage of spiritual maturation for us. We cannot be full of the Spirit when we are full of self, and we will be full of self until we mourn the hapless state of the self to which we cling. Our mourning gives way to joy in Christ, and as life, love, and joy are drawn from Christ, meekness of soul turns our hearts toward God. In detachment from this world, we are able fully to enjoy it, but if we truly achieve this freedom of life, how quickly we are reminded of its transient and superficial nature. The soul then turns to

---

[19] Matthew 5:6a.

longing for that which cannot be taken from us, that which will not die, that which is eternal and eternally blessed: the righteousness of God. We long for God's justice, God's wisdom, and God's judgment, all of which are given to us by the Holy Spirit Who now has the freedom to move strongly within us, shedding the light of God in our hearts and minds.

As God's righteousness takes root in our souls, we become merciful[20] for that is how God is. God's wisdom, God's judgment, God's righteousness are *merciful*. To be merciful is to have compassion for those who are wounded, to extend leniency and forgiveness to sinners, to offer kindness to the undeserving, and to give aid and assistance to those suffering hardship. This is what God has done for all human beings in Jesus Christ, and ever so slowly as we mature as Christians, we are being shaped and formed into His likeness – truly in His likeness. To be Christian is to be like Christ. Although we call ourselves Christian, we are so far from this state when we simply believe, but if we humble ourselves and submit to the guidance and correction of the Holy Spirit, this amazing, supernatural transformation starts taking place, slowly, sometimes quickly, but always ongoing. To be merciful as God is merciful is to bring healing, salvation, and redemption to a deeply wounded and sinful world.

The reward for being merciful is receiving mercy. If we live to an old age, praying and seeking God, the fact remains that we still will need to be shown mercy. As long as we live in these earthly bodies, we struggle against the sinful nature of death within us. When the time comes and we meet God face to face, His final mercy of giving us full acceptance into His Kingdom is more reward than we ever deserved. As St. John Chrysostom said in his homily on the Beatitudes, "The reward at first glance appears to be an equal reimbursement, but actually the reward from God is much greater than human acts of goodness. For whereas we ourselves are showing mercy as human beings, we are obtaining mercy from the God of all. Human mercy and God's mercy are not

---

[20] Matthew 5:7a.

the same thing. As wide as the interval is between corrupted and perfect goodness, so far is human mercy distinguished from divine mercy."[21]

When we have attained meekness of soul – a calm soul, unruffled and unangered in pride and insecurity by others and by self, when we thirst for the wisdom, justice, and righteousness of God, when we cannot but be merciful to others because we have received so much mercy ourselves, our hearts are purified by the life-giving fire of the Holy Spirit. The many sins and conceits, the fears, shame, and guilt that plague us, the selfishness and egotism that are the mark of human nature give way to purity of heart. *"Blessed are the pure in heart, for they will see God."*[22] It is possible to see God this side of death. We see Him in a mystical sense, but we still see Him with our eyes, eyes that can see beyond the physical and into eternity because the soul is pure. Yet, this is a singular experience, the rare state of mystical bliss in which the light and glory of God are visible to our physical eyes, and we experience God in a tangible manner.

Purity of heart, however, also allows us to see God in spite of the sin, death, and evil around us, to discern His presence and ministry in places where He seems absent. An abbreviated version of the Breastplate (Lorica)[23] of St. Patrick read:

> Christ with me, Christ before me,
> Christ behind me, Christ in me,
> Christ under me, Christ over me
> Christ to the right of me, Christ where I lie down,
> Christ where I sit, Christ where I rise,
> Christ in the heart of everyone who scrutinizes me,
> Christ in the mouth of everyone who speaks to me,
> Christ in every eye that sees me,

---

[21] St. John Chrysostom, The Gospel of Matthew, Homily 15.4, *Ancient Christian Commentary on Scripture, Vol. 1A,* ed. Thomas Oden, (Downers Grove, IL: IVP, 2001), 85.

[22] Matthew 5:8.

[23] A Lorica is a mystical hymn or prayer of protection and grace sung repeatedly throughout the day. St. Patrick's Lorica is famous, at least in its abbreviated form, and is translated from Gaelic with few variations. The full Lorica is quite lengthy and equally beautiful.

Christ in every ear that hears me.

Only the pure in heart move through this world knowingly surrounded by Christ, ever in His presence wherever we are and with whomever we may be. Our words and actions are filtered through Christ's gracious presence and ministry to all we meet. With such purity of heart, we will see God, both in and through us and at work in the world.

Daily Reflection and Meditation

On the Heels of Poverty and Mourning

Have you ever mourned your sin, as in, grieved that you are such a sinful person? If so, when, and if not, why?

_____

_____

_____

_____

_____

St. Symeon believed that tears of sorrow for the grief and death we caused Christ to partake of are necessary for salvation and purity of heart, going so far as to say we should not be able to receive Holy Communion without weeping.[24] Why do you suppose he would suggest such an idea?

_____

_____

_____

_____

_____

Although God desires us to live free of guilt, the recognition of the limits of human goodness should cause remorse and humility in us. Do you recognize this? If so, what difference does it make to you?

_____

---

[24] *Discourses*, Paulist Press, p. 70.

What are sources of anger, pride, and insecurity in your life? Why do these things cause anger, pride, and/or insecurity?

Do you yearn for God's wisdom and judgment? If so, how does this yearning express itself in your life?

How do you think you would experience life if you met each person and situation with the purity of heart given by the Holy Spirit? What do you think that would be like?

From Glory into Glory

Peace and Persecution

"Blessed are the peacemakers, for they will be called sons of God."[25] To put this Beatitude in context, I want us to consider Jesus' words to His disciples, "Peace I leave with you; My peace I give you. I do not give to you as the world gives. Do not let your hearts be troubled and do not be afraid."[26] Peace is a fragile state and never long-lasting in this world. The peace of which Christ speaks is the eternal peace of wholeness and holiness, of union between God and one another. This peace between God and us and between other human beings and us is not of our world, but from the Kingdom of God. Worldly peace is measured by human standards of justice and power, not by true unity. Peace is more a state of co-existence than of communion. That is the peace of this world. Jesus knew this.

> Do you think I came to bring peace on earth? No, I tell you, but division. From now on there will be five in one family divided against each other, three against two and two against three. They will be divided, father against son and son against father, mother against daughter and daughter against mother, mother-in-law against daughter-in-law and daughter-in-law against mother-in-law.[27]

Likewise, in talking about the future of the disciples, Jesus said,

> You will hear of wars and rumors of wars, but see to it that you are not alarmed. Such things must happen, but the end is still to come. Nation will rise against nation, and kingdom against kingdom. There will be famines and earthquakes in various places.[28]

Our generation tends toward a dangerous naiveté about human nature. We wrongly believe we can build a just and peaceful world. That is not so. The world in which we live is the world of sin and death, not justice and peace. This is the world that Jesus Christ came to save because it needs to be saved. To imagine that human schemes and human negotiations can bring about world peace is a wonderful idea, but however lovely this sentiment, it is not grounded

---

[25] Matthew 5:9.
[26] John 14:27.
[27] Luke 12:51-53.
[28] Matthew 27:6-7.

in reality. Certainly, we can and should work toward peaceful co-existence, but we also should fight against evil.[29]

A peacemaker in the likeness of Jesus Christ is one who truly reunites and reconciles people to God and to one another. Such peace is built not upon human efforts, but through the Crucified Lord Who left His peace with His disciples. This is divine peace, a holy communion and reconciliation born of godly love. Christ Jesus bought peace for us at the price of the Cross, and that is peace between the Father and fallen humanity. Therefore, the Christian peacemaker is reconciling the world to God by divine grace and mercy. This is our priestly task: to stand as mediators between God and humankind, laying down our lives for others that they may know God.[30] One cannot be a peacemaker unless we are pure in heart, and one cannot be pure in heart without inevitably being a peacemaker as well. Because God desires peace with the world, when our souls are purified of sin and we are filled with the Holy Spirit, we also desire peace between God and the world. In short, we cannot but seek to reconcile others to God. As Paul wrote,

> All this is from God, who reconciled us to Himself through Christ and gave us the ministry of reconciliation: that God was reconciling the world to Himself in Christ, not counting men's sins against them. And He has committed to us the message of reconciliation. We are therefore Christ's ambassadors, as though God were making His appeal through us. We implore you on Christ's behalf: Be reconciled to God.[31]

The ultimate act of peace was actually an act of horrific violence. Peace with God was achieved through the Cross of Christ, and we are "His ambassadors" in the world. As Jesus Christ is the Son of God, when we take up the ministry of reconciliation – reconciling the world to God – we live as the sons and daughters of God. Our reward is not earthly peace, but becoming

---

[29] This topic is far broader than can be adequately addressed in this context. Let me simply say, the time and place for war exist in the world in which we live. Pacifism in the Name of Jesus Christ, while admirable, implies Jesus did not mean what He said about wars and division. Likewise, when we think we can avoid all conflict, we deny the reality of the breadth and depth of the sinful nature of *all* human beings, as well as the very real presence of evil in our world.

[30] This would be in contrast to laying down our lives and allowing evil to conquer.

[31] 2 Corinthians 5:18-20.

true children of our eternal Father. As the Son of God brought peace between God and the world, living as peacemakers carrying the message of reconciliation to God into the world gives us the divine reward of being a child of God. We must be pure in heart to be a peacemaker. We live as peacemakers only when our passion is for the divine redemption of others through reconciliation to God. There is no personal gain or benefit to reconciling others to God. To the contrary, reconciling the world to God will lead to persecution.

"Blessed are those who are persecuted because of righteousness, for theirs is the Kingdom of heaven. Blessed are you when people insult you, persecute you and falsely say all kinds of evil against you because of Me. Rejoice and be glad, because great is your reward in heaven, for in the same way they persecuted the prophets who were before you."[32] Finally, we have come full circle. "Blessed are those who are persecuted because of righteousness, for theirs is the Kingdom of heaven." But this is the same reward as is offered to the poor in spirit. If we begin the journey of following Jesus Christ, the Holy Spirit will move us through stages of growth and purification until finally we are sufficiently like Christ that we are a threat to the world. At least, the Holy Spirit will work in us as long as we submit to Him. If we truly seek the poverty of spirit that enables us to know God and to follow Him, eventually we will be like Christ – truly Christian – in every way.

As Jesus Christ told His disciples, "If the world hates you, keep in mind that it hated Me first. If you belonged to the world, it would love you as its own. As it is, you do not belong to the world, but I have chosen you out of the world. That is why the world hates you."[33] None of us actually wants to be hated by the world, but then, neither did Christ. Would that the world had embraced God in our midst and lived happily ever after… But that would be a different world from our own. Our world crucified the Son of God, and if we follow Him, one day, the world will hate us as well. By that time, we will have reached such fellowship with God that persecution is preferable to denial. If we can understand that the persecution and hate are born of sin and ignorance of the love of God, then we will more readily forgive and seek peace – be a peacemaker.

---

[32] Matthew 5:10-12.
[33] John 15:18-19.

However, the world is what it is. Each new generation of Christians is given the same opportunity to become truly like Christ. We are invited to know God, to draw close to Him and be blessed by Him. God has opened the gates of eternity so we might draw life from His Kingdom while still in the world. If we do so, we will become ourselves, more glorious than anything we ever imagined, but as creatures of life, we will attract the wrath of sin and death.

From Glory into Glory

Daily Reflection and Meditation

Peace and Persecution

How do Christian peace and worldly peace differ?

_____
_____
_____
_____
_____

What do you think a peacemaker in the likeness of Christ looks like in our world today?

_____
_____
_____
_____
_____

Can you reconcile the call to the life of a peacemaker with the reality of war? If so, how?

_____
_____
_____
_____
_____

Have you ever experienced negative reactions or responses from others because you are a Christian? If yes, describe such an occasion. How did you respond?

_____
_____
_____
_____
_____
_____

If faced with a serous cost for Christian discipleship, how do you think you respond, and why?

_____
_____
_____
_____
_____
_____

Is Christian faith worth persecution? Explain your answer.

_____
_____
_____
_____
_____
_____

From Glory into Glory

Our destiny is so easy to see. It is right before our eyes, but we do not recognize it. If we progress in spiritual maturation, we will be transformed, and we will be like Christ. The revelation of human destiny ought to be obvious, but it is not.

> After six days Jesus took with Him Peter, James and John the brother of James, and led them up a high mountain by themselves. There He was transfigured before them. His face shone like the sun, and His clothes became as white as the light. Just then there appeared before them Moses and Elijah, talking with Jesus.[34]

The Man Jesus was transfigured and revealed as the Son of God in the glorious, uncreated divine light. Now reconsider the quote from St. Symeon's *Discourses* above:

> Where there is unfeigned humiliation there is also the depth of humility, and where there is humility, there is also the enlightenment of the Spirit. Where there is the enlightenment of the Spirit there is the outpouring of the light of God, there is God in the wisdom and knowledge of His mysteries. Where these mysteries are to be found, there is the Kingdom of heaven and the experience of the kingdom and the hidden treasures of the knowledge of God, which include the manifestation of poverty of spirit. Where poverty of spirit is perceived, there is also the sorrow that is full of joy. There are ever-flowing tears that purify the soul that loves these things and cause it to be completely filled with light.[35]

A human being fully alive in God, one who is his Father's glory, is the transfigured human seen on the side of Mount of Christ's Transfiguration. That is finally what it means to be like Christ, to be one in whom God is made manifest. Personally, I do not think we achieve such glory in this world, but I am convinced we can make progress in that direction. But we must remember that our movement toward our destiny is also a movement from selfishness and sin to selflessness and purity of heart. To be like Christ is to love the world of which we are no longer a part, and to have a heart broken for those who are

---

[34] Matthew 17:1-3.
[35] ibid.

not reconciled to our Father. Our glorious destiny is beyond our comprehension, although we know it is not a singular destiny, but union with the Triune God and communion with all the saints. We are wise to heed the advice of C.S. Lewis on this matter.

> It may be possible for each to think too much of his own potential glory hereafter; it is hardly possible for him to think too often or too deeply about that of his neighbor. The load, or weight, or burden of my neighbor's glory should be laid on my back, a load so heavy only humility can carry it, and the backs of the proud will be broken. It is a serious thing to live in a society of possible gods and goddesses, to remember that the dullest and most uninteresting person you can talk to may one day be a creature which, if you saw it now, you would be strongly tempted to worship, or else a horror and a corruption such you now meet, if at all, only in a nightmare. All day long we are, in some degree, helping each other to one or other of these destinations. It is in the light of these overwhelming possibilities, it is with the awe and circumspection proper to them, that we should conduct all our dealings with one another, all friendships, all loves, all play, all politics. There are no *ordinary* people. You have never talked to a mere mortal. Nations, cultures, arts, civilizations – these are mortal, and their life is to ours as the life of gnat. But it is immortals whom we joke with, work with, marry, snub, and exploit – immortal horrors or everlasting splendors. This does not mean that we are to be perpetually solemn. We must play. But our merriment must be of that kind (and it is, in fact, the merriest kind) which exists between people who have, from the outset, taken each other seriously – no flippancy, no superiority, no presumption. And our charity must be real and costly love, with deep feeling for the sins in spite of which we love the sinner – no mere tolerance, or indulgence that parodies love as flippancy parodies merriment. Next to the Blessed Sacrament itself, your neighbor is the holiest object present to your sense. If he is your Christian neighbor, he is holy in almost the same

way, for in him also Christ *vere lavitat*[36] – the Glorifier and the Glorified, Glory Himself, is truly hidden.[37]

Christian salvation is so much more than accepting Jesus, being forgiven, and getting into heaven when we die. It is life beyond anything we can begin to comprehend, offered to us by the eternal God Who was, Who is, and Who always shall be. Because He is Who He is – the Great I AM – we are infinitely more than we know ourselves to be, children made in the Image of the "one God and Father of all, who is over all and through all and in all."[38] As such, may we remember and live the hymn and prayer of David for the rest of our lives:

Praise be to You, O LORD, God of our father Israel,
    from everlasting to everlasting.
Yours, O LORD, is the greatness and the power
    and the glory and the majesty and the splendor,
    for everything in heaven and earth is Yours.
Yours, O LORD, is the kingdom; You are exalted as head over all.
Wealth and honor come from You; You are the ruler of all things.
In Your hands are strength and power to exalt and give strength to all.
Now, our God, we give You thanks,
    and praise Your glorious name.

But who am I, and who are my people, that we should be able to give as generously as this? Everything comes from You, and we have given You only what comes from Your Hand.[39]

---

[36] Latin meaning "truly hides."
[37] C.S. Lewis, *The Weight of Glory*, (NY: Harper One, 2001), 45-46, emphasis as in original.
[38] Ephesians 4:6.
[39] 1 Chronicles 29:10b-14.

www.ingramcontent.com/pod-product-compliance
Lightning Source LLC
Chambersburg PA
CBHW060528100426
42743CB00009B/1463